First published in Great Britain in 2016 on behalf of:
Nuclear Risk Insurers Ltd, 5th Floor, 18 St Swithin's Lane, London, EC4N 8AD

Published by:
RMC Media – www.rmcmedia.co.uk
6 Broadfield Court, Sheffield, S8 0XF
Tel: 0114 250 6300

Author: Andrew Maddix with Martin Edwards
Design: Richard Abbey
Proof-reader: Christopher Brierley

Printed and bound in Great Britain by:
CPI Colour Ltd – www.cpicolour.co.uk
108-110 Beddington Lane, Croydon, Surrey, CR0 4YY
Tel: 020 8688 7500

A CIP catalogue record for this book is available from the British Library.

ISBN: 978-1-907998-27-0

Andrew Maddix

The Nuclear Chef

Celebrating 60 years of NRI

Contents

I would like to dedicate this book to my mother and father, Antony and Inell Maddix. I would like to thank them for their love and support, and for instilling in me that with hard work and determination, I can achieve anything I put my mind to.

I would like to give special recognition to three people whose help has been instrumental in my completing this book: my wife Mellonie Maddix, Yoland Brown, events management and decorator (ykbrown@yahoo.co.uk); and Marvalyn Chambers.

Finally, a big thank you to Nuclear Risk Insurers Ltd and to my colleagues for giving me the opportunity to produce this book.

Foreword

I once asked Andy if he'd ever considered producing a cookery book. The answer came back no. But there was a twinkle in his eye. Nothing more was said until recently, when as a team, we were discussing how might NRI recognise our 60th year since formation. What would help us capture the essence of NRI?

For NRI's 50th celebrations a book had been produced containing certain historical documents. There was the Management Agreement; a list of the original membership and minutes of the inaugural meeting of the Executive Committee on 30th August 1956. Highlights in the minutes included approval from the Chairman's office to advance the British Insurance (Atomic Energy) Committee £500.00 until the Committee had a formal constitution. It was further noted that subscriptions had reached £12,463,275 Material Damage and £5,410,307 Public Liability at each station. And there was a report that lightning conductors had been fitted to certain buildings at Calder Hall.

So what would we do to celebrate 60 years? Perhaps some photos, a vase or a tie. Or a 60th year umbrella – after all, NRI is based in London! We decided that The Nuclear Chef would be the answer.

Andy has cooked for just about every pool, client, member, broker, consultant and adviser that NRI has hosted in London over the past ten years or so. Our lunches, served in the dining room at our offices are an important feature of the NRI identity and enable confidential discussion.

We've had some fun developing The Nuclear Chef. Andy has worked tirelessly to get the recipes right, and he's put his creative and artistic flair into it. We must thank everyone who has contributed to our book too, including all those who have donated their time or ingredients.

We hope that our clients, members, colleagues and friends worldwide will enjoy The Nuclear Chef.

Mark Popplewell
Managing Director

Foreword

The nuclear industry is a bit of a mystery to me. On one point however, I can be certain. The people who work in it are very well fed. This book is proof, were it needed, of that. The past and present of Nuclear Risk Insurers feature in this superbly-illustrated and well-told story of Andy Maddix, the Nuclear Chef.

Manchester-born and well-travelled, Andy loves rooting around the early morning markets in London for the prime ingredients which go into the delicious dishes he serves up for the company's clients and their associates, who come to their London HQ from around the world. In this book, he highlights some of his dishes that have become firm favourites. Enjoy!

Brian Turner CBE

1.

NUCLEAR RISK INSURERS LTD

In 1956, with the emergence of the UK civil nuclear power industry, the British Insurance (Atomic Energy) Committee was born.

The Nuclear Pool was established by insurance companies and Lloyd's syndicates to manage the insurance of nuclear third party liability and material damage risks of nuclear installations.

Now known as the Nuclear Risk Insurers Limited (NRI), it has played a key role in the growth of nuclear insurance internationally.

Many of the international pools which have followed have been modelled on the UK pool. This has led to NRI enjoying excellent relationships with those pools.

It has also opened the doors to the availability of extremely well-rated insurance security for nuclear operators across the world.

Today NRI represents one of the largest single blocks of risk transfer insurance capacity in the world, at £600m, and is one of the oldest nuclear insurers globally.

It is led by Managing Director Mark Popplewell and employs two active underwriters and three nuclear technical experts and has expertise through a large network of key industry individuals and consultants.

NRI's journey over the last 60 years
The mid-1950s saw the birth of the nuclear age. Calder Hall, the UK's first full-scale nuclear power station, developed for civil purposes, was opened at Sellafield in Cumbria by the Queen in 1956.

With the rise of nuclear energy came the call from the industry and the UK Government to insure the associated risks. At the same time similar nuclear developments were happening elsewhere in the world, most notably in the United States and France. Similar demands were being made on insurers in those countries.

Insurers found themselves facing two problems: How best to provide cover for the emerging nuclear industry in general and how to provide protection for the general public without exposing insurers' solvency margins to the potentially catastrophic losses that could arise from widespread radioactive contamination.

In order to provide adequate insurance for the nuclear energy industry it was recognised that the insurance market had to do things differently. The sheer nature and size of the nuclear industry meant it was beyond the resource of any one national market or individual insurer.

When British Insurance (Atomic Energy) Committee launched almost every insurance company and Lloyd's syndicate in the UK was asked to join.

In total there were 82 insurance companies and 137 Lloyd's syndicates that joined originally and in turn six brokers helped put the cover in place and came up with £26m – an impressive figure by 1950s standards. Today, 60 years on and NRI manage £600m of capacity with just over 26 members.

In 2003 Nuclear Risk Insurers Ltd (NRI Ltd) was formed in its current structure as a company limited by guarantee of its members. NRI is managed via a Pool Management Agreement (PMA); it is also a Lloyd's coverholder and is regulated by the Financial Conduct Authority (FCA) and finally it adheres to the Standard Rules adopted by the Global Pooling system.

The insurance companies and Lloyd's underwriters who support NRI have delegated their authority to NRI Ltd's board of directors and in turn the board has delegate authorities to the permanent staff of NRI Ltd.

NRI is proud of the difference it makes in its field.

NRI acts as an observer for the insurers at the meetings of the Organisation for Economic Cooperation and Development's (OECD) Nuclear Energy Agency Group of Governmental experts on third party liability in the field of nuclear energy and it provides a lecturer to the OECD's International School of Nuclear Law.

NRI is also the permanent Secretary to the General Purposes Committee (GPC) of the Pooling system – the GPC acts as a mechanism for development of best practice arranging seminars, such as the annual Nuclear Pools Forum where current topics that affect all Pools, including Engineering inspection and Claims management are discussed.

How NRI operates – mechanics

NRI Ltd is a company limited by guarantee, a business structure suited to non-profit organisations.
The insurers who pool their capacity for nuclear risks into NRI are commonly known as the British nuclear insurance pool.

Member insurers can provide insurance capacity to one or more classes of business, which are underwritten by NRI and include: material damage, nuclear liability and nuclear transit liability.

NRI uses its capacity to provide suitable insurance cover not only for the nuclear sites in the UK but reciprocally to reinsure other nuclear sites around the world in association with similar international pools.

The major part of the British nuclear pool's income is from the reinsurance accepted from other nuclear pools where NRI's capacity enables it to play an important role.

NRI covers risks including property in all parts of the nuclear fuel cycle, such as the nuclear fuel handling and radioactive waste management industries, construction work on nuclear energy sites and transport liabilities and research centres using nuclear substances.

The exchange of common account reinsurance between national pools provides access to the worldwide insurance capacity.

Being part of this means NRI has the capacity to fully insure its clients.

Nuclear insurance markets have developed across the world in line with nuclear energy growth.

NRI has helped a number of countries over the last 60 years to develop their own pooling mechanisms such as Canada, South Africa and Romania.

What makes NRI unique?

NRI's clients are found in every corner of the globe. Wherever there is a nuclear industry it can be expected that NRI is involved in some capacity.

From Russia to China, Japan to South Africa and the United States, NRI is a unique business and is extremely proud of its diverse client-base and the service it provides.

NRI welcomes clients from all over the world to its London offices. This led in 1988 to the appointment of it's first corporate chef and the installation of a full kitchen.

The visits from clients, brokers, international pools, NRI members and all the associated advisers, consultants and experts and the dining experience they enjoy when at the London offices are a huge part of NRI's brand and what makes it special.

Current head chef Andy Maddix is known by NRI's contacts around the world. The relationship adds to the personalised service which NRI has been proud to offer for the last six decades.

Nuclear installations offer high engineering risk management standards. This is why with every new client NRI has a view that it will insure them. If they cannot get insurance they will not be able to operate.

This has led to an incredibly strong link between the nuclear industry and NRI.

For the last 60 years the two have supported each other. NRI has been able to provide extremely stable insurance protection for its clients whilst at the same time the industry represents a low frequency exposure – but the severity is high.

Its engineers and underwriters spend their lives thinking about nuclear insurance.

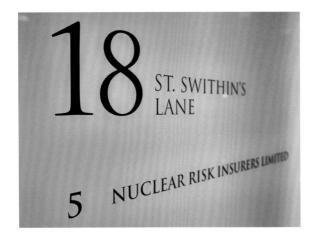

NRI is ready and primed to pay out on a nuclear liability claim should one arise. The company operates on a 'when it happens' rather than 'if it is going to happen' basis.

A considerable amount of time and money is spent maintaining its claims handling system. NRI has lawyers and loss adjusters on retention. The backing and security of NRI is of the highest quality in the global insurance market.

The company is proud of its work with the government. As the representative of the London insurance market on nuclear insurance matters, NRI maintains contact with the government and frequently contributes to discussions on a wide variety of nuclear matters like current or proposed legislation in the nuclear industry.

The future of nuclear and how NRI will play its part

In 2016 the nuclear energy market is in a very different place to that in 1956 when NRI established. The switch on of nuclear power in Calder was followed by a further nine nuclear power stations being built across Britain over the next ten years. Today, the emerging nuclear energy countries are predominately South Korea, China, India, Middle East and Africa.

NRI is maintaining and developing strong relationships with the local pools that operate in those countries while operating from the UK.

In the UK nuclear is an aging industry. Many nuclear power stations are reaching the end of their lives and decommissioning work is taking place.

NRI is working with its clients to insure and offer the right support and protection through those procedures.

Despite the decommissioning operations 2016 has also seen the announcement of the country's first nuclear power station for a generation.

In the year that NRI celebrates its 60th anniversary it also celebrates the UK signing an £18bn contract with France and China to build Hinkley Point C. EDF Energy is building the power station in Somerset which marks an exciting time for NRI. NRI will work closely to make sure the plant has the right protection and cover needed and this year NRI has diversified and started insuring the construction insurance for nuclear businesses via a Binding Authority.

Previously, NRI commenced cover at various stages as fuel arrived onto site. It shows how NRI is moving with the changing times and making sure it can offer the right cover and the protection for its clients.

The nuclear industry is changing and the risks are changing with them but NRI will continue to provide the right products and services to help the industry operate.

2.

ANDREW MADDIX

First there was Molecular Gastronomy. Now there's the Nuclear Chef.

I love to see the puzzled look on people's faces when I tell them what I do. Am I perhaps pioneering a new form of sous vide cooking in a reactor? Or working on a practical way of harnessing atomic fusion in the kitchen?

Far from it. In actual fact, I am Executive Chef at Nuclear Risk Insurers, a major nuclear insurer based in the City of London. They're the people who are on standby should the unthinkable happen. Because of that, we're visited by leading figures in the industry worldwide – from China, Japan, South Africa, wherever there are nuclear power facilities. It's my job to feed them, which we set out to do in style. The guests are served the same standard of food that would be on the menu in an outstanding restaurant.

So an average working day could see me providing private dining during a board meeting to a client lunch appointment for a Canadian nuclear power operator.

It's a far cry from where I started out many years ago in Manchester at the time I was learning my trade. It's been a fascinating journey that has taken me across the world and granted me the opportunity earlier in my career of cooking for prime ministers and world leaders in Downing Street.

I often say that I have never done a day's work in my life. By that I mean I regard cooking as a pleasure, not a chore.

Every chef can recall key moments of discovery, events that have influenced them and helped determine their career direction, and I'm no exception. For me it was my first encounter with truly fresh fruit: mangoes, pineapples and other exotic fruit still ripening and ready to be picked. They were a commonplace sight in Jamaica, where I spent two years at the age of ten, but oh… the flavour! It was quite unlike anything you could buy back in England.

There'd be coffee and cocoa growing in the fields and my aunt would use cocoa beans to make the most amazing hot chocolate with nutmeg in it. The taste was indescribable. I'd never come across anything like it. I was seeing organic food being produced, because lots of it – such as the chickens and pigs that were running around the houses – was there in front of your eyes.

My grandfather had something of a reputation as a chef on the island at the time. His speciality was catering for events in the village such as weddings. He'd make huge quantities of curry, his speciality, cooked in the Jamaican style. This is lighter than Indian curries, and doesn't include cumin or coriander.

My interest in cooking now firmly rooted, the family and I returned to the UK in 1976. And it wasn't long before I set out to develop my interest in food.

Every chef can also point to an individual who has influenced his or her chosen path. In my case it was Micky Brennan in Manchester. An old-school Irish chef, he taught me about the business as well as kitchencraft. He would, for example, take me along on his trip to the markets at 6am, where he'd show me the glorious fresh riches on show, like the mounds of langoustines, Dublin Bay prawns and lobsters.

When he thought I was up to the task, he would give me £50 and dispatch me to the markets to do some buying. On my return he would look at my purchases and take the time to tell me where I'd done well and where I could have done better. It was a grounding in the art of budgeting which would stand me in good stead for the rest of my career.

But there was one test of dedication that everyone had to go through. It was soon my turn to wash up for a month. The theory was that if you still wanted to work as a chef after that, you must be serious about it – and there was the added bonus that the employers would pay for you to go to college. My initiation was over.

Or maybe not quite. On one particular day the owner of the chain of restaurants Micky and I worked for asked me to help out with a staff shortage at one of the kitchens. I volunteered straight away. I told the boss I'd start at 2pm to give me plenty of time to do my mise en place – the preparation of ingredients which is the most essential tool in a chef's armoury. Underlying this ritual of a few hours chopping, slicing and general activity, is the idea that every component of a dish is at hand and ready when it comes to the actual cooking. It's then just a case of assembling the finished article ready to be sent out of the kitchen.

In a reassuringly relaxed way he insisted I needed nothing like that amount of time on mere preparation. Half of that would be ample.

Service came that evening, and with it a hundred or so diners. Very soon my meagre supply of mise en place began to shrink alarmingly and then it ran out completely. I stopped the whole kitchen. I was besieged by other chefs who were brought to a halt because the starters hadn't been sent out. Their steaks were overcooking and the situation looked desperate. I retreated to the gents.

There was only one alternative to going back to face a kitchen full of angry chefs. I tried to climb out of the window. When it proved too tight a squeeze I returned to the fray and toughed it out. Somehow we got through the service.

The moral of that story is to remember the scouts' motto. Be prepared.

The following years took me to America and various corners of England. Every new place brought with it an opportunity to learn more. But I also found out that unforeseen difficulties have a nasty way of ambushing you, as I found out on one memorable occasion.

Following in my grandfather's steps, I agreed to provide the catering for a friend's wedding. The guest list, at 500, was a long one but there was plenty of notice so we prepared accordingly. We took care of hiring the staff, sourcing the wine and ordering the food. Everything was fine until the night before the wedding, when my brother let it drop that he too had been invited.

"Really? When was that?" I asked. "Today" came the answer.

This set alarm bells ringing, so I immediately called the groom. "About the wedding catering," I asked, "It was for 500 guests, wasn't it?"

My blood ran cold at the reply.

"I don't know."

It turned out my friend had been randomly inviting people who he met during the last few weeks before the big day. Apparently in his African homeland it's regarded as a great honour to have a large guest list at one's wedding. His best estimate was now just over 800.

It was my worst nightmare. There were guests standing up because there wasn't enough seating at the tables. It was chaotic. In the end I made the available menu stretch to feed all 800 with that great lifesaver, a hastily-thrown together curry. But that was an experience I'd never like to repeat.

Whether it was the shock of that episode or not, I eventually decided that my future lay in cooking for directors' dining rooms. That meant a move to London and working days in places like the headquarters of the major merchant banks and financial institutions. The style of cooking was exceptional and no expense was spared. Here at last was the chance to express my creativity.

The company I was working for had other prestigious contracts, among them Downing Street. After several months of security checking which left no stone unturned, I finally received clearance to work at this iconic address.

My five years there was the time of Prime Ministers Blair and Brown, and it was an experience like no other.

I'd work in one of Number 10's two kitchens cooking food for the country's top politicians and visiting heads of state. There aren't many places where you can be going about your daily routine and see the likes of Nelson Mandela walking past!

We were allowed in most places apart from the private quarters. The experience was unreal. I'd have to pinch myself to think that, for instance, I was sitting in a chair where Winston Churchill had sat. In all, it seemed a very long way from where I started out at New Hall Green School and my family home in Manchester's Moss Side.

I'm still working at a major British institution, one that's celebrating 60 years being the best in the business. The recipes I've chosen in this book are the product of a lifetime's love affair with cooking, and I present them here as a fitting tribute to a great global player. Happy birthday NRI.

3.

BREAD

Makes 1 loaf

1 tablespoon good quality honey
(e.g. Manuka)
185ml warm milk (oat or almond milk
can be used)
2 teaspoons sugar
Half tablespoon salt
Half tablespoon active dry yeast

1 tablespoon vegetable oil
1 egg
140g strong white bread flour
140g wholewheat flour
50g sunflower seeds, plus more for
sprinkling on top

Sunflower seed bread

1. In a food mixer combine honey, milk, sugar, salt, yeast, oil and egg.

2. Add flour and sunflower seeds and mix just until dough starts to pull away from the sides of the bowl.

3. Pour dough into a lightly greased bowl, cover and let it rise until doubled in size (approximately two hours).

4. Shape risen dough into an oval and place in a lightly greased 8 x 4-inch loaf tin. Cover and let it rise until doubled, about 30-40 minutes.

5. Preheat oven to 190°C/375°F/Gas mark 5.

6. Brush the top of the loaf with a little vegetable oil and sprinkle sunflower seeds on top. Bake loaf for about 35-40 minutes.

7. Place on cooling rack to cool.

8. When cool slice and serve.

Makes 1 loaf

400g rye flour (dark or light)
350g strong plain flour
1 teaspoon demerara sugar
2 teaspoons salt
150g 100 per cent All-Bran
2 tablespoons caraway seeds, crushed
2 teaspoons instant coffee powder
2 teaspoons onion powder

Half teaspoon fennel seeds, crushed
2 x 7g packs active dry yeast
625ml water
Splash of balsamic vinegar
60ml dark molasses
30g unsweetened chocolate
75g butter plus more for greasing
1 teaspoon cornflour
125ml cold water

Russian black bread

1. Mix together rye and plain flour.

2. In a large bowl, thoroughly mix two-thirds of the flour mixture with sugar, salt, cereal, caraway seeds, coffee powder, onion powder, fennel seeds and undissolved yeast.

3. In a saucepan, blend 625ml water, vinegar, molasses, chocolate and butter. Heat liquid mixture over low heat until liquids are very warm (butter and chocolate do not have to be melted). Gradually add heated liquid mixture to dry ingredients and beat (with electric mixer) for two minutes at medium speed.

4. Add 80g of the flour mixture. Mix at high speed for a further two minutes. Stir in enough additional flour to make a soft dough.

5. Turn dough on to a lightly floured board. Cover and rest for 15 minutes.

6. Knead dough until smooth and elastic (about 15 minutes); dough may become sticky.

7. Place dough in a large greased bowl, turning dough to grease the top. Cover bowl and place in a warm, draught-free place to rise until doubled in bulk.

8. Turn out onto a lightly floured board and divide dough in half. Shape each half into a ball, about five inches in diameter. Place each ball into the centre of a greased 8-inch round cake tin. Cover and leave to rise in a warm place until doubled in size (about an hour).

9. Preheat oven to 180°C/350°F/Gas mark 4.

10. Bake for approximately 45 minutes, or until done.

11. Meanwhile, combine cornflour and cold water. Cook over medium heat, stirring constantly, until mixture starts to boil. Continue cooking mixture for one minute, stirring constantly. As soon as bread is baked, brush cornflour mixture over top of loaves.

12. Return bread to oven and bake for about three minutes till glaze is set. Remove loaves from pans and cool on wire racks.

13. When cool, slice and serve.

Makes 1 loaf

500g strong white bread flour, plus
extra for dusting
7g salt
50g caster sugar
10g instant yeast
140ml warm full-fat milk (can
substitute half oat or soya milk)
5 medium eggs
250g unsalted butter, softened, plus
extra for greasing
5g poppy seeds

Brioche

1. Put the flour into the bowl of a mixer fitted with a dough hook. Add the salt and sugar to one side of the bowl and the yeast to the other. Add the milk and eggs and mix on a slow speed for two minutes, then on a medium speed for a further 6-8 minutes, until you have a soft, glossy, elastic dough.

2. Add the softened butter and continue to mix for a further 4-5 minutes, ensuring the butter is thoroughly incorporated. The dough will be very soft.

3. Tip the dough into a bowl, cover and chill overnight till it is firm enough to shape.

4. Grease a 25cm round deep cake tin with butter. Take your brioche dough from the fridge. Tip it onto a lightly floured surface and fold it on itself a few times to knock out the air. Divide it into nine equal pieces.

5. Shape each piece into a smooth ball. Put the eight balls of dough around the outside of the tin and the final one in the middle. Cover with clingfilm and leave to prove for 2-3 hours, or until the dough has risen to just above the rim of the tin.

6. Heat your oven to 190°C/375°F/Gas mark 5.

7. When the brioche is proved, sprinkle with the poppy seeds and bake for 20-30 minutes.

8. Check with skewer inserted in centre.

9. When fully baked remove from oven, place on wire rack and cool.

Makes 1 loaf

500g strong white bread flour,
plus extra for dusting
15g fresh yeast
2 teaspoons salt
1 teaspoon sugar
2 tablespoons olive oil
Handful black olives, sliced

Olive oil bread

1. Place flour into a mixing bowl and crumble in the fresh yeast. Rub into the flour as you would with butter when making pastry, then add the salt and sugar.

2. Boil the kettle and measure 100ml into a jug. Top up with cold water to 300ml. Water should be hand hot.

3. Add the oil.

4. Make a well in the centre of the dry ingredients and pour in the liquid all at once. Mix quickly using your hands to make a soft and slightly sticky dough.

5. Sprinkle the work surface with flour and tip out the dough. Knead by stretching it away from you, then folding it in half towards you and pushing it away with the heel of your hand.

6. Give it a quarter turn and repeat.

7. When the dough is smooth, put it back into the mixing bowl, cover with a tea towel and leave to rest for an hour. The dough is ready when it springs back when you press it with your finger.

8. Tip dough onto a floured surface and knead to remove air bubbles. Shape into a round, place on an oiled baking sheet and slash top twice with sharp knife. Scatter olives on top.

9. Cover and rise for 30 minutes.

10. Preheat oven to 220°C/425°F/Gas mark 7.

11. Bake for 30-35 minutes until browned and crisp.

12. Cool and serve.

Makes 1 loaf

Heaped teaspoon active dry yeast
375ml water, at room temperature
500g strong plain flour, plus extra for
dusting
160g cornmeal, plus more for
sprinkling
1 tablespoon salt
150g toasted pumpkin seeds

You will need:
Baking stone

Pumpkin seed bread

1. Dissolve a good pinch of the yeast in 250ml of the water. Stir in 300g of the flour. Cover with clingfilm and stand overnight in a warm place.

2. Dissolve the remaining yeast in 60ml of water.

3. Put the cornmeal in a large heatproof bowl. Bring the remaining 65ml of water to a boil, stir it into the cornmeal and let cool.

4. Stir in the salt, both yeast mixtures and the remaining 200g of flour to make a soft dough. Transfer to a floured surface and knead until smooth and elastic (about 15 minutes).

5. Knead in the pumpkin seeds. Return the dough to the bowl, cover with clingfilm and let it rise for one hour.

6. Turn the dough out onto a work surface and gently fold four times. Return the dough to the bowl, cover and prove until doubled in size.

7. Sprinkle a baking sheet with cornmeal.

8. Turn the dough out onto a work surface and divide in half. Shape each half into a round loaf. Set the loaves on the baking sheet and let rise until doubled in size.

9. Set a baking stone on the middle rack of the oven and preheat the oven to 240°C/475°F/Gas mark 9 (stone can take up to 45 minutes to heat).

10. Fill a roasting pan with hot water and set it on the bottom rack.

11. Make three slashes in the tops of the loaves, transfer them to the stone and bake for ten minutes.

12. Reduce the oven temperature to 230°C/450°F/Gas mark 8 and bake for a further 20 minutes.

13. Once baked, remove from oven and cool on rack, then slice and serve.

Olive oil, for greasing
400g strong white bread flour, plus
extra for dusting
100g strong wholemeal flour
10g salt
12g fast-action dried yeast
370ml cool water (made from one
part boiling, one part chilled)

Mixed flour baguettes

1. Lightly oil a two-litre square plastic container with olive oil.

2. Thoroughly combine white and wholemeal flour with salt then add yeast. Place into bowl of a freestanding mixer fitted with a dough hook. Add three-quarters of the water and begin mixing on a slow speed. As the dough starts to come together, slowly add the remaining water, then continue to mix on a medium speed for 5-7 minutes, until you have a glossy, elastic dough. Tip the dough into the prepared tub. Cover and leave for an hour, or until at least doubled in size.

3. Dredge a linen couche (canvas for proofing bread) with flour and lightly dust the work surface with flour.

4. Carefully tip the dough onto the work surface. Handle it gently so you can keep as much air in the dough as possible. The dough will be wet to the touch but still lively.

5. Divide the dough into four pieces. Shape each piece into an oblong by flattening the dough out slightly and folding the sides into the middle. Then roll each up into a sausage – the top should be smooth with the join running along the length of the base.

6. Now, beginning in the middle, roll each piece of dough gently with your hands – concentrating on the backwards and forwards movement – until about 30cm long.

7. Lay a baguette along the edge of the linen couche and pleat the couche up against the edge of the baguette. Place another baguette next to the pleat. Repeat the process until all four baguettes are lined up against each other with a pleat between each.

8. Cover the baguettes with a clean tea towel and leave for an hour, or until the dough has at least doubled in size and springs back quickly if you prod it lightly with your finger.

9. Preheat the oven to 240°C/475°F/Gas mark 9 and put a roasting tray in the bottom of the oven to heat up.

10. When the baguettes are risen, remove them from the couche and dust lightly with flour. Slash each one four times along its length on the diagonal, using a very sharp knife. Transfer to a large baking tray.

11. Fill the heated roasting tray (in the oven) with hot water, to create steam, and put the bread into the oven.

12. Bake for 20-25 minutes, or until the baguettes are golden-brown and have a slight sheen.

13. Cool on a wire rack.

170g self-raising wholemeal flour
170g plain flour, plus extra for
kneading
Half teaspoon salt
Half teaspoon bicarbonate of soda
290ml buttermilk, plus extra if
needed

Irish soda bread

1. Preheat the oven to 200°C/400°F/Gas mark 6.
2. Tip the flours, salt and bicarbonate of soda into a large mixing bowl and stir.
3. Make a well in the centre and pour in the buttermilk, mixing quickly with a large fork to form a soft dough. Add additional buttermilk if needed.
4. Turn onto a lightly floured surface and knead briefly.
5. Form into a round and flatten the dough slightly before placing on a lightly floured baking sheet.
6. Slash the top with a knife and bake for about 30 minutes or until the loaf sounds hollow when tapped.
7. Cool on a wire rack.

Variations on this recipe:
Substitute 90ml buttermilk with soya, oat or almond milk.
Add 75-100g sunflower or pumpkin seeds to the dry mixture (adding a little extra milk to form a soft dough).

Makes 1 loaf

For the focaccia:
400g strong white bread flour, plus extra for dusting
100g fine ground semolina flour
Half teaspoon sea salt
1 x 7g sachet dried yeast
Half tablespoon golden caster sugar
300ml water, lukewarm
Olive oil, for greasing
Good drizzle of extra virgin olive oil

For the balsamic topping:
2 red onions, finely sliced
A few sprigs of fresh thyme, leaves picked
2 tablespoons olive oil
6 tablespoons good quality balsamic vinegar
Sprinkle of sea salt

For the basil and cherry tomato topping:
1 bunch fresh basil, leaves picked
1 large handful ripe cherry tomatoes, halved
Sea salt
Freshly-ground black pepper
Drizzle of extra virgin olive oil
Splash of white wine vinegar
2 cloves garlic, peeled and sliced

For the three cheese and rosemary topping:
30g dolcelatte cheese
1 small log goat cheese (125g)
30g Parmesan cheese, grated
1 sprig of fresh rosemary, leaves picked
Black pepper
Good drizzle of extra virgin olive oil
Sprinkle of sea salt

Three flavour focaccia

1. Combine the plain and semolina flour with a half tablespoon of sea salt in a large bowl. Make a well in the middle. Add the yeast and sugar to the lukewarm water, and mix with a fork. Leave this for a few minutes and, when it starts to foam, slowly pour it into the well, mixing as you go.

2. As soon as all the ingredients come together, knead vigorously for around five minutes until you have a smooth, springy, soft dough.

3. Lightly oil a large bowl with some olive oil and transfer the dough to the bowl. Dust with a little extra flour, cover with a tea towel and leave to rise in a warm place for 30 minutes until doubled in size.

4. Preheat oven to 220°C/425°F/Gas mark 7.

For the balsamic topping:

1. Fry the sliced onions and thyme leaves in two tablespoons of olive oil over a low heat for about five minutes.

2. Add the balsamic vinegar, reduce for a minute or two, then cool.

For the basil and cherry tomato topping:

1. Roughly chop the basil leaves and pop them into a bowl with the cherry tomatoes. Season with salt and pepper, a drizzle of extra virgin olive oil and a tiny splash of white wine vinegar. Add the garlic and mix it all.

To bake:

1. As soon as the dough has risen knock it back by turning out onto a lightly floured surface and kneading for a couple of minutes, then place on a lightly greased baking tray. Press down roughly on top of the dough to make lots of rough dips and wells.

2. Divide the onion and the tomato toppings over two-thirds of the focaccia.

3. For the three cheese and rosemary topping, break up the dolcelatte and the goat's cheese over the remaining third of the focaccia. Sprinkle over the grated Parmesan and rosemary leaves and season with pepper.

4. Finish with a good drizzle of extra virgin olive oil and a sprinkle of sea salt. Set aside to prove for a further 20 minutes then bake for 20 minutes, until golden on top and soft in the middle.

4.

FISH

Serves 4
300g fresh linguine
400g prepared small squid
4 tablespoons extra virgin olive oil,
plus extra for drizzling
300g large peeled raw prawns with
tails and shells on
Half red and half green chilli, diced
3 garlic cloves, finely crushed

Bunch of spring onions, sliced
150g yellow baby tomatoes, halved
150g red baby tomatoes, halved
50g red vein sorrel or wild rocket
Sea salt and freshly-ground black
pepper, to taste
Juice of 1 lemon
Parmesan (optional)

Simple linguine with garlic, squid and prawns

1. Cook the linguine in lightly salted boiling water for about six minutes (after this keep checking approximately every 30 seconds) or until al dente. Drain, reserving a little of the cooking liquid.
2. While linguine is cooking, slit one side of each squid pouch and open them out flat. Using a sharp knife, score the insides using a diamond pattern, then cut the flesh into 5cm pieces. Set aside the squid pieces with the tentacles.
3. Heat the oil in a large frying pan over a high heat. Add the squid and cook for two minutes or until golden and lightly caramelised. Lift out and set aside. Add the prawns, chillies, garlic and spring onions and cook for two minutes, then add the tomatoes. Continue to cook for a further couple of minutes or until the prawns are cooked through. Add the squid and toss lightly.
4. Stir the red vein sorrel and a splash of the reserved pasta cooking liquid through the linguine. Add the seafood and tomato mixture.
5. Season well, add the lemon juice and divide between four bowls. Drizzle with the extra oil to serve and add Parmesan if required.

"Beautiful lunch, thank you."
Matt Waters, Barclays

"Delicious!!!"
Zuo Huiqiang, Chinese pool

Serves 4
30g unsalted butter
300g celeriac, peeled and chopped
into 1cm cubes
200ml milk
75ml double cream
2 bulbs of fennel
2 large banana shallots, peeled and

roughly chopped
1 bay leaf
25g smoked bacon, in a slice
100ml mandarin purée
50ml Pernod
A few parsley and thyme stalks
Vegetable or light chicken stock
4 x 130g fillets wild sea bass, boned

and trimmed, skin on
Sea salt and black pepper, to season
2 tablespoons olive oil
Lemon juice, to taste
Glaze balsamic vinegar (or other
good quality balsamic)
Scarlet cress, for garnish

Roasted wild sea bass with celeriac purée and braised fennel

To make the celeriac purée:

1. To make the purée, melt a small knob of butter (approx. 20g) in a saucepan, add the celeriac and cook over a medium-high heat until starting to brown a little (about five minutes).

2. Pour over the milk and cream, and season well – the celeriac should be just covered, so add more milk if needed. Bring to a simmer, cover and cook for 15 minutes or until tender. Drain, reserving the cooking liquid, and transfer to a food processor. Blend until smooth, then sieve into a clean saucepan, pushing the celeriac through with the back of a spoon or spatula. Add a little of the cooking liquid to loosen the purée if needed, and taste for seasoning. Reserve.

Prepare the fennel:

1. Trim any stalks and leaves from the fennel. Take a thin slice from the base of the each bulb, then chop them vertically in half, leaving in the root and saving the trimmings.

2. Put the fennel in a small gastronom (or small ovenproof dish) with the trimmings, shallots, bay leaf, bacon, mandarin purée, Pernod and herbs, adding enough cooking stock so that the fennel is just covered.

3. Cover with a cartouche of buttered greaseproof paper, then cook at 180°C/350°F/Gas mark 4 for 45 minutes. Take out the fennel, strain the liquor and reduce in a pan to about 150ml. Put the fennel back in the reduced liquor and reserve.

To serve:

1. Heat a non stick frying pan with 1 tablespoon olive oil. Season the fish fillets with sea salt and black pepper. Cook skin-side down until crisp, turning it over when about two-thirds cooked. Add 10g butter, then a squeeze of lemon juice. Baste the skin side until golden brown. When still slightly underdone, remove from heat.

2. Meanwhile in a separate pan, caramelise the fennel in a tablespoon of oil. Heat the celeriac purée, arrange the fish, celeriac, fennel and balsamic vinegar on a hot plate. Garnish with scarlet cress and serve immediately.

"Delicious."
Tomohiro Ichiki, Japanese pool

Serves 4

16 baby leeks

3 tablespoons extra virgin olive oil

4 x John Dory fillets approximately 175g each, skin left on

1 large knob butter, melted

Sea salt and black pepper, to season

For the potatoes:

675g Maris Piper potatoes, peeled and quartered

50g butter

100-150ml double cream

Salt and ground white pepper

Finely-grated zest and juice of 2 blood oranges

For the Hollandaise sauce:

2 tablespoons water

2 egg yolks

225g butter

Juice of half a lemon

Pinch of cayenne pepper

Salt

John Dory fillets with baby leeks and Hollandaise sauce

1. Make the potatoes first. Boil the potatoes in salted water till tender, approximately 20-25 minutes, before draining off the water. The potatoes can now be mashed, adding the butter a little at a time, along with the preferred quantity of double cream. Season with salt and ground white pepper.

2. Boil together the orange zest and juice, allowing it to reduce in volume by at least three-quarters. Stir the juice into the potatoes. These can now be rewarmed just before serving.

3. While the potatoes are cooking, prepare the Hollandaise sauce by putting the water and egg yolks into a glass bowl set over a pan of simmering water, making sure the base of the bowl is not touching the water. Whisk until pale, thick and creamy.

4. Remove the bowl from the pan and gradually whisk in the butter until thick. Then whisk in the lemon juice, cayenne pepper and salt. Set aside.

5. Preheat the grill to high. Cook the leeks in boiling salted water for 2-3 minutes until just tender but still al dente. Drain and refresh under cold water, then dry out on kitchen paper.

6. Heat a ridged cast iron griddle over a high heat. Brush with a little oil then place the leeks diagonally across it and grill for slightly less than a minute on each side so that they get nicely marked with diagonal lines. Remove the leeks from the griddle and place on hot plates.

7. Cut each John Dory fillet diagonally across into two similar-sized pieces. Brush on both sides with the melted butter and season well with salt and pepper. Lay the fillets skin-side up on a lightly-greased baking sheet and grill for four minutes. Remove and serve with leeks, creamed potatoes and Hollandaise sauce.

"Just great."

Emil Gavrilov, Bulgarian pool

Serves 6
1kg fish fillets, including salmon,
smoked haddock and white fish (cod,
haddock or pollock)
125g butter
1 medium onion, diced
2 cloves garlic, crushed
150ml white wine

Smoked haddock trimmings
560ml milk
280ml double cream
200g plain flour
1 tablespoon Dijon mustard
Handful of chives, parsley and
tarragon, chopped
1kg Maris Piper potatoes

300g sweet potatoes
Salt and pepper, to season
1 egg yolk
A little lemon juice
Handful of fresh breadcrumbs
A little grated Parmesan

Andrew Maddix's fish pie

1. Remove the skin from the fish and pin bone. Cut into bite-sized pieces, reserving the skin of the smoked haddock for the sauce.

2. Heat 25g butter in a saucepan, add the onion and garlic, then sweat until softened. Add the white wine and the smoked haddock and cook to burn off the alcohol. Stir in the milk and cream and bring to just under the boil, then take the pan from the heat, pass the contents through a sieve into a bowl and keep hot.

3. Melt the rest of the butter in a heavy saucepan, add the flour and cook over a low heat, stirring well for five minutes. Pour the hot infused milk into the pan and whisk vigorously until the mixture is smooth and thick as the flour has cooked out. Whisk in the mustard, add the chives, parsley and tarragon and adjust the seasoning. Preheat oven to 180°C/350°F/Gas mark 4.

4. Peel the potatoes and cook in boiling salted water until tender. Drain in a colander, mash with a ricer and season with salt and pepper. Stir in the egg yolk, mixing thoroughly, and spoon the mash into a piping bag.

5. To assemble, spoon a little of the sauce into the bottom of each of four pie dishes. Arrange a selection of fish on top of the sauce. Season with salt and pepper and a squeeze of lemon juice

6. Completely cover with sauce then pipe on the mash. Mix together the breadcrumbs and Parmesan and sprinkle evenly over the pies. Place the pie dishes on a baking sheet and cook for around 20 minutes until the top is golden brown and the centre of each pie is hot. Serve immediately.

"Great meal."
Colleen DeMerchant, Canadian pool

Serves 4

For the pea purée:
400g frozen peas

For the risotto:
80g unsalted butter
Half onion
2 shallots
1 garlic clove, finely chopped

350g Arborio rice
Small glass dry white wine
1.2 litres/2 pints hot fish stock
Salt and freshly-ground black pepper
25g Parmesan, freshly-grated

For the fish:
4 x 100g portions of haddock fillet,
skinned and pin-boned

Flour, for dusting
Salt, to season
1 tablespoon cooking oil
Knob of butter
1 heaped teaspoon sesame seeds
1 heaped teaspoon poppy seeds
1 tablespoon sesame oil

Haddock with pea risotto and toasted sesame and poppy seeds

For the pea purée:

1. Bring a large pan of salted water to the boil and blanch the peas for three minutes.
2. Add the peas to a blender along with a little water. Blitz, adding more liquid in small quantities as needed. Blend for no more than a couple of minutes, until a fairly thick, smooth purée has been achieved.
3. Tip the purée into a fine sieve and use the back of the ladle to push it through – this will give you a silky-smooth finish. Set aside.

For the risotto:

1. Heat the butter in a large, heavy-based saucepan and add the onion, shallots and garlic. Fry over a gentle heat for 2-3 minutes, until softened.
2. Stir in the rice and coat in the butter. Pour in the wine and simmer, stirring, until the liquid has been absorbed. Add a ladleful of the stock and simmer, stirring again, until the liquid has been absorbed. Continue adding the stock in this way until all the liquid has been absorbed and the rice is plump and tender. Add butter, and salt and pepper.
3. Shortly before the risotto is ready, stir in the pea purée and serve when the risotto has reached the required consistency.
4. Serve with freshly-grated Parmesan.

For the fish:

1. Lightly dust the skinned sides of the haddock fillets with flour and season with salt.
2. Heat the cooking oil in a frying pan and add the fillets, floured side down. Cook for four minutes until golden brown. Add the knob of butter then turn and continue to fry for a further two minutes.
3. The sesame and poppy seeds can be used natural, as they are, or toasted to a golden brown under a hot grill for a richer and nuttier finish.
4. Put risotto on a plate, place haddock on top and garnish with Parmesan.

"Excellent as always."
Alexandru Havris, Romania

Serves 4
Mangetout
450g turbot
Flour, for dusting
1 tablespoon olive oil
Knob of butter
Half a lime
Affilla cress (optional)

For the parsnip purée:
450g parsnips, peeled and thinly sliced
2 garlic cloves, thinly sliced
120ml heavy cream
120ml whole milk
2 tablespoons unsalted butter
Sea salt

For the herb dressing:
1 tablespoon of each of the following, chopped: parsley, dill, chives, tarragon and chervil
100ml olive oil
3 tablespoons truffle oil

Turbot on parsnip purée with a fresh herb dressing

For the parsnip purée
1. Bring parsnips, garlic, cream, milk, and butter to a boil in a medium saucepan. Reduce heat, cover, and simmer until parsnips are very soft (10-15 minutes).
2. Uncover and cook until liquid is reduced by half (about five minutes). Season with salt.
3. Purée in a blender until smooth.

For the herb dressing:
1. Reserve a level teaspoon of each herb to garnish the mangetout.
2. Place all the remaining chopped herbs in a liquidiser.
3. Heat the olive and truffle oils in a small saucepan until just warm. Pour on top of the herbs and liquidise to a smooth purée. Strain through a sieve.

For the mangetout:
1. To cook in advance, put mangetout into boiling salted water till cooked. Drain and refresh in cold water.
2. To reheat, plunge into boiling water for ten seconds.

For the turbot:
1. Cut the turbot into four equal portions, checking the flesh has been pin-boned. Score the skin with a sharp knife, cutting just two or three lengths.
2. Season the flesh side with salt and pepper and the skin side with salt only. Lightly dust the skin side with flour.
3. Heat a frying pan and add the olive oil. Once bubbling, place the fillets in skin-side down and cook for about five minutes. Add knob of butter.
4. Turn the fish and remove pan from the heat. The heat contained in the pan will finish the cooking process.

To serve:
1. Warm the mangetout then drench them with five tablespoons of the fresh herb dressing. Add the reserved chopped herbs and juice from the half lime. Adjust the seasoning with salt and pepper.
2. Spoon the warm parsnip purée into the centre of a plate. Arrange the mangetout and add the dressing.
3. Sit the turbot on top of the parsnip purée. Garnish with Affilla cress (if using) and serve.

Serves 4

4 mackerel fillets, pin-boned
Salt and pepper, to season
Flour, for dusting
1-2 tablespoons cooking oil
Knob of butter

For the gooseberry and ginger sauce:
225g gooseberries
125g onions, chopped
285ml red wine vinegar
225g soft brown sugar
1 teaspoon salt

15g stem ginger
Half teaspoon cayenne pepper

Red mackerel with gooseberry and ginger sauce

1. To make the sauce, gently cook the gooseberries in a little water until they have softened.

2. Add the chopped onions and vinegar, cooking for five minutes or so.

3. Next, add all other ingredients, boiling gently until some of the liquid has evaporated and the mixture has a slightly thick consistency. Leave to cool.

4. Season the mackerel fillets with salt and pepper then dust the skinned sides with a little flour.

5. Heat the oil in a large frying pan and place the fillets in, floured side down. Fry for up to four minutes, then add the knob of butter. Turn the fillets in the pan and remove from the heat.

6. Leave to bubble in the warm pan for a minute or two during which time the fish will finish cooking and its texture will relax.

7. The fillets can now be dressed with the gooseberry and ginger sauce.

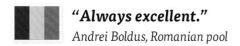

"Always excellent."
Andrei Boldus, Romanian pool

Serves 4

14 medium white asparagus spears
14 medium green asparagus spears
4 x 175g portions salmon trout fillet,
pin-boned with skin on
Salt and pepper
Flour, for dusting
2 tablespoons cooking oil

Knob of butter, plus more for brushing
Coarse sea salt (optional)
Shiso cress (optional)

For the sauce:
2 tablespoon water
2 egg yolks
225g butter

Juice of half a lemon
Pinch of cayenne pepper
Salt, to taste
64ml juice from blood orange
1 teaspoon orange zest

Crispy salmon trout with warm blood orange sauce

1. Prepare the sauce by putting the water and egg yolks into a glass bowl set over a pan of simmering water, making sure the base of the bowl is not touching the water. Whisk until pale, thick and creamy.
2. Remove the bowl from the pan and gradually whisk in the butter until thick. Then whisk in the lemon juice, cayenne pepper and salt. Add orange juice and orange zest, fold, then set aside in a warm place.
3. Trim the spiky 'ears' from along the asparagus stalks and break or cut the grey-white stalk base away, keeping the spears uniform length.
4. Season the salmon trout fillets with salt and pepper and lightly flour the skins side only.
5. Put a large pan of salted water on to boil.
6. Heat the cooking oil in a large frying pan and place the fillets in skin-side down. Fry on medium-hot heat for six or seven minutes, taking care not to shake or move the fish. Allow the skins to fry and crisp.
7. Turn the fillets, add the knob of butter and remove the pan from the heat. The remaining residual heat will continue to cook the fish for a further few minutes, keeping the flesh moist and buttery.
8. After turning the salmon trout, plunge the asparagus tips into the large saucepan of rapidly boiling salted water. Cook for just two or three minutes until tender – no more than four minutes.
9. Lift the spears from the pan, drain well and brush with butter to add more flavour and create a shine.
10. Place the spears side by side on a plate and season with a sprinkle of coarse sea salt if desired. Sit the crisp salmon on top of the warm sauce.
11. Garnish with shiso cress (optional) and serve.

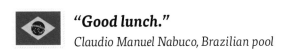 **"Good lunch."**
Claudio Manuel Nabuco, Brazilian pool

Serves 4

550g whitebait
Sunflower oil, for deep frying
75g plain flour
Half teaspoon smoked paprika
1 lemon, cut into wedges to serve

For the tartare sauce:
200ml mayonnaise
70g capers, drained and chopped
70g gherkins, drained and chopped
1 small shallot, finely chopped
Squeeze of lemon juice
3 tablespoons fresh parsley, chopped
Flaked sea salt and freshly-ground
black pepper

Deep fried whitebait with lemon tartare sauce

1. To make the tartare sauce, mix together all of the ingredients in a small bowl and serve straight away or store in the fridge until needed.
2. Wash the whitebait in plenty of cold water, then drain and shake vigorously in a colander.
3. Heat oil for deep frying to 190°C/375°F/Gas mark 5.
4. Put the flour, smoked paprika and salt into a large bowl, mix together well and add the whitebait. Toss together until they are all well coated, then lift them out and shake off the excess flour.
5. Deep-fry the fish in batches for about three minutes until crisp.
6. Drain briefly on kitchen paper then tip into a large serving bowl and sprinkle with the chopped parsley.
7. Serve with the lemon wedges.

"Delicious."
Laura Wells, W R Berkley 1967

Serves 4
800g squid
Half teaspoon pink peppercorns
Half teaspoon black peppercorns
1 teaspoon coriander salt or sea salt flakes
1-2 tablespoons rapeseed oil
Half small red scotch bonnet, thinly sliced (seeds removed, if you prefer –
this is a very hot pepper)
2 spring onions, sliced

To garnish:
3 teaspoons sweet soy sauce
3 teaspoons roasted sesame oil
Pinch of sea salt
Daikon salad leaves or salad rocket

Stir-fried salt and pepper squid

1. Prepare the squid (see linguine recipe on page 52).
2. Season the squid with pink and black peppercorns and coriander salt. Leave for five minutes.
3. For the sauce, whisk together the soy sauce, sesame oil and salt. Set aside.
4. Heat a heavy-based pan over a high heat. Add half the oil and half the squid and pan fry for two minutes, until lightly coloured. Tip on to a plate, then cook the remaining squid in the same way.
5. Return the first batch of squid to the pan and toss together for about ten seconds, then add the scotch bonnet and spring onions and toss together very briefly.
6. Divide the squid between four serving plates, garnish with the salad leaves and drizzle on the warm sweet soy sauce dressing. Serve immediately.

"The finest food."
Ingrid Carlou, Mexican pool

Serves 4
Hollandaise sauce (see John Dory recipe on page 54)
300ml milk
300ml water
3 bay leaves
2 slices onion
6 black peppercorns
4 x 100g pieces of thick undyed smoked haddock fillets
1 tablespoon white wine vinegar
4 eggs
2 English muffins
4 large handfuls of baby spinach
1 teaspoon nutmeg (or mace)
Salt and pepper, to season
Coarsely-crushed black peppercorns and a little chopped chives, to garnish

Smoked haddock with spinach and egg

1. Make the Hollandaise sauce (as per the John Dory recipe on page 54) and keep it warm over a pan of water.
2. Bring the milk and the water to the boil in a pan. Add the bay leaves, onion, peppercorns and smoked haddock. Bring back to a simmer and poach for four minutes. Lift the fish out and put on to a plate. Peel off the skin and keep warm.
3. Put about 5cm of water to the boil in a medium-sized pan, add the vinegar and reduce it to a gentle simmer. Break the eggs one at a time and poach for three minutes.
4. Meanwhile, slice the muffins in half and toast them until lightly browned. Lift the poached egg with a slotted spoon and drain briefly on kitchen paper.
5. Place the muffin halves on to four warmed plates.
6. Pan fry spinach in a hot pan for a minute and season with nutmeg, black pepper and salt.
7. Place spinach on top of muffin and top with haddock and poached eggs. Spoon over the Hollandaise sauce and a sprinkling of crushed black pepper and chopped chives.

"Good lunch."
Zuzana Repova, Slovakian pool

Serves 4
2 x 350g pieces of prepared thick
monkfish fillet
Salt, to season
900g russet potatoes (purple or
Maris Piper)
4 tablespoons olive oil

4 onions, thinly sliced
2 cloves garlic, chopped
125g butter
Salt and pepper, to season
85ml extra virgin olive oil, plus extra
to serve
Balsamic vinegar

Sea salt flakes, coarsely-crushed
black pepper and lemon thyme, to
serve

Roast monkfish with onions and purple potatoes

1. Preheat the oven to 200°C/400°F/Gas mark 6.

2. Season the monkfish with some salt and set it aside for 15 minutes.

3. Peel potatoes and cut into half-inch slices. Place sliced potatoes in a pot and cover with water. Bring to a boil. Allow to boil for a couple of minutes, then drain and set aside.

4. Heat a large ovenproof skillet over medium-high heat. Pour in olive oil, then add onions and garlic. Sauté until lightly caramelised (8-10 minutes). Stir in garlic and sauté until onions are deep brown and garlic is soft. Transfer mixture to a bowl.

5. Place back on stove over low heat. Melt butter, then cover bottom of pan with a third of the potatoes. Season with salt and pepper. Cover potatoes with half of onion mixture. Cover with half of remaining potatoes and season with salt and pepper. Spread with the rest of onion mixture. Cover with remaining potatoes, and season with more salt and pepper.

6. Bake in the oven for 10-12 minutes, or until potatoes are tender and browned on top.

7. Pat the monkfish dry on kitchen paper, add to the pan and sear for three minutes or so, turning it three or four times until nicely browned on all sides.

8. Transfer the pan to the oven and roast for 10-12 minutes until the fish is cooked through but still moist and juicy in the center. Remove from the oven, cover with foil and set aside for five minutes.

9. To serve, cut the monkfish into thick slices.

10. Remove potatoes from the oven and place on to four warmed plates. Put the monkfish on top. Put your thumb over the top of the bottle of extra virgin olive oil and drizzle a little of it around the outside edge of each plate. Do the same with the balsamic vinegar and then sprinkle around a few sea salt flakes and some coarsely-crushed black pepper and lemon thyme.

"Great meal."
Julian Gomez del Campo, Spanish pool

Thanks so much for this great lunch."
Yannick Le Gonidec , Apave

Serves 4
300g spaghetti
35g butter
65g sliced pancetta
1 finely-chopped shallot
20 medium-sized clams

100ml white wine
200ml milk
200ml double cream
Salt and freshly-ground white pepper
1 tablespoon chopped parsley

Clams with spaghetti

1. Cook spaghetti for approximately seven minutes in boiling salted water until al dente, and set aside.
2. Melt the butter in the pan, add the pancetta and fry over a medium heat until golden. Add the shallot and cook gently until softened.
3. Add the clams, white wine, milk and cream and cook till the clams open (approximately four minutes).
4. Add cooked spaghetti to clams.
5. Season to taste with salt and pepper, garnish with parsley and serve.

"Fabulous food, thanks."
Achim Jansen-Tersteegen, German pool

Serves 4
20 razor clams, washed
Olive oil
Truffle oil
Salt and pepper
Lemon wedges, to serve (optional)
Lemon cress

Razor clams

1. Heat a large heavy-based frying pan over a high heat until very hot. Add a little olive oil and a single layer of the clams, hinge-side down.
2. As soon as they have opened right up, turn them over so that the meats come into contact with the base of the pan and cook for about a minute until lightly browned.
3. Turn the clams back over, drizzle over a little truffle oil, lightly season and put on a warmed serving plate. Serve with a lemon wedge, and any juices from the pan. Garnish with lemon cress.
4. Repeat the process with any remaining clams.

"Very nice, chef."
Martin Chang, Taiwanese pool

Serves 4

1.75kg mussels, cleaned
50g unsalted butter
1 medium onion, finely chopped
50ml dry white wine
1 tablespoon coarsely chopped parsley

Moules mariniere

1. Put the mussels, butter, onion and white wine into a very large pan. Cover and cook over a high heat for three to four minutes, shaking the pan every now and then, until the mussels have opened.
2. Spoon the mussels into four individual warmed bowls. Add the parsley to the remaining juices and pour over the mussels.

NOTE: *Do not use all the juice as grit may gather at the bottom.*

 **"Lovely Andrew."**
Nikola Rendic-Miocevic, Croatian pool

Serves 4

For the fish stock (makes
approximately 500ml):
125g fish trimmings (you can include
fish heads, bones and skin)
2 leeks
Half a bulb fennel
1 carrot

Handful fresh parsley
100ml dry white wine

For the brill:
50g butter
1 shallot, finely chopped
50ml dry white wine
12 green-lipped mussels

4 x 225g brill fillets
3 tablespoons double cream
1 tablespoon tarragon, chopped
Salt and freshly-ground black pepper

Steamed fillet of brill with green-lipped mussels

For the fish stock:

1. Rinse fish bones well with cold water.
2. Roughly chop leeks, fennel, carrot and parsley and place into a small pot.
3. Add the fish.
4. Pour in the white wine, then add enough cold water to cover the fish and vegetables (about half a litre).
5. Bring almost to a boil over high heat (do not let it come to a boil). Reduce heat to low and cook at a bare simmer, skimming any foam that rises to surface. This should take about 10-15 minutes.
6. At the end of cooking time, remove the stock from the heat and strain, discarding the fish and the vegetables.

For the fish:

1. Put 300ml of the fish stock into a small pan and boil it rapidly until reduced to half volume.
2. Melt a knob of the butter in a medium-sized pan. Cut the rest into small pieces. Add the shallot to the pan and cook gently for five minutes, until soft. Add the wine and simmer until reduced to about 2 tablespoons. Add the reduced fish stock and keep warm.
3. Remove mussels from the shells, clean them and retain four of the deeper shells for serving. Put aside.
4. Season the fish fillets on both sides with a little salt and lay them on a heatproof plate. Place a trivet in a large pan and pour in about 25cm of water. Bring to a vigorous simmer. Then put the plate on the trivet, cover the pan and steam for four minutes. Lift the fish out of the steamer and pour the juices from the plate into the sauce. Cover the fish and keep it warm.
5. Bring the sauce to a gentle simmer, add the mussels and their juice and poach for two minutes. Lift them out with a slotted spoon and keep them warm with the brill.
6. Add the cream to the sauce and simmer vigorously for three minutes. Then whisk in the remaining butter, a few pieces at a time, to form an emulsified sauce. Stir in the tarragon and season with black pepper and a little salt if necessary.

Serves 4
600ml olive oil
4 x 175g pieces salmon trout fillet
1 tablespoon extra virgin olive oil
1 large cucumber, peeled and thinly
sliced

1 tablespoon chopped dill, plus a few
sprigs to garnish
1 tablespoon chives
2 teaspoons white wine vinegar
Sea salt
White pepper

Salmon trout poached in olive oil with cucumber and dill

1. Pour a thin layer of the olive oil into a pan just large enough to hold the pieces of salmon trout side by side. Season the fish on both sides with a little salt, put it in the pan and pour over the rest of the oil – it should just cover the salmon.

2. Heat the oil very slowly, ensuring that the temperature is consistent throughout the pan, to approximately 60°C.

3. Now take the pan off the heat and leave it in a warm place for 25 minutes to continue the cooking process. If temperature falls below 60°C, return to heat to maintain temperature.

4. Shortly before the fish is ready, heat the extra virgin olive oil in a large frying pan. Add the cucumber slices and toss over a medium heat for one minute. Add the dill, chives, vinegar and a little salt and pepper.

5. Place equal measures of cucumber between the serving plates. Gently remove the fish from the oil, making sure there is no excess, and arrange on top of the cucumber.

6. Pour the oil off into a jug. What you should be left with is the juice from the fish, which will be at the bottom of the pan. Drizzle the juice around the edge of each plate, sprinkle the fish with a few sea salt flakes and garnish with a sprig of fresh dill.

"Great food. Can I take Andy?"
Gerry Thomas, Imperial College

Serves 4
40g cream crackers
250g fresh white crab meat
200g lobster meat
1 egg, beaten
2 tablespoons mayonnaise
1 tablespoon English mustard
1 tablespoon lemon juice

1 teaspoon cayenne pepper
1 teaspoon brandy
2 tablespoons parsley, chopped
4 tablespoons melted butter
A dash of Worcestershire sauce
A dash of Tabasco sauce
Salt and freshly-ground white pepper

For the fine herb sauce:
50ml sherry vinegar
55g butter
1 plum tomato, skinned, seeded and diced
1 teaspoon chopped mixed herbs (tarragon, chives, chervil, parsley)

Crab cakes with a fine herb sauce

1. Put the cream crackers into a plastic bag and crush into fine crumbs with a rolling pin.
2. Put the crab and lobster into a bowl and add just enough of the cracker crumbs to absorb any moisture.
3. Break the egg into a small bowl and whisk in the mayonnaise, mustard, lemon juice, Tabasco, brandy, Worcestershire sauce, salt and pepper
4. Gently fold this into the crab and lobster mixture. Stir in the parsley.
5. Shape the mixture into eight 7cm patties, put them on a plate, cover with clingfilm and chill for at least an hour.
6. Heat the butter in a large frying pan. Add the fishcakes and cook over a medium heat for two to three minutes on each side until crisp and golden.

For the sauce:
1. Boil the vinegar in a small pan until reduced to about two tablespoons. Add the butter, diced tomato, chopped tarragon, chives, chervil, parsley and some salt and pepper to taste and gently warm through.
2. Serve with the fishcakes.

"Delicious lunch, many thanks."
Jacqueline Woods, London

"Truly excellent meal chef."
Peter Glynne-Percy, Mitsui Sumitomo Insurance

Serves 4
2 x 750g cooked lobsters
2 tablespoons rapeseed oil
1 onion, chopped
3 garlic cloves, crushed
2 stem ginger bulbs, roughly chopped
1 green chilli, deseeded and chopped
1 red chilli, deseeded and chopped
3 tablespoons good quality curry paste
1 teaspoon ground cumin
1 teaspoon ground coriander

Curried lobster

1. Preheat the oven to 150°C/300°F/Gas mark 2.
2. Remove the meat from the cooked lobsters. Place the shells on a baking tray and warm them through in the oven.
3. Heat the oil in a heavy-based frying pan and add the onion, garlic, red and green chilli, cumin and coriander. Fry for five minutes.
4. Add the stem ginger and curry paste and fry for a further two minutes.
5. Fold in the lobster meat and cook gently until it has heated through.
6. Spoon the mixture back into the lobster shells and serve.
7. This dish goes well with a green salad and spicy naan bread.

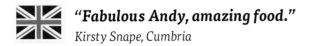
"Fabulous Andy, amazing food."
Kirsty Snape, Cumbria

Serves 4

550g unpeeled headless raw prawns
2 tablespoons white wine vinegar
1 teaspoon salt
1 teaspoon mixed peppercorns (pink, black and green)
1 teaspoon garam masala
1 teaspoon ground cumin
1 tablespoons ground coriander
4 tablespoons groundnut oil
1 red onion, chopped

3 garlic cloves, sliced
2cm fresh root ginger, finely chopped
3 tablespoons ground almonds
400ml coconut milk
150ml water
1 teaspoon saffron powder
1 small scotch bonnet, diced
1 teaspoon salt
2 tablespoons fresh coriander, chopped

Spicy prawns

1. Peel the prawns, leaving the last tail segment in place.
2. Mix the prawns with the vinegar and a teaspoon of salt. Set aside for five minutes.
3. Meanwhile, grind the peppercorns and combine with garam masala, ground cumin and ground coriander.
4. Heat the oil in a heavy-based pan. Add the onion, garlic and ginger and fry gently for five minutes. Stir in the ground spices and fry for two minutes. Add the ground almonds, coconut milk, water, saffron powder, scotch bonnet and a teaspoon of salt. Bring to a simmer and cook for five minutes.
5. Add the prawns and cook for approximately four minutes.
6. Stir in the fresh coriander and serve with boiled rice.

"Excellent meal, thank you."
Simon Clegg, Lloyd's

Serves 4

250g salted cod, boneless and skinless
2 tablespoons rapeseed oil
2 cloves garlic, peeled and crushed
1 medium onion, sliced
1 scotch bonnet pepper
Quarter of a medium red sweet bell

pepper
2 shallots
2 sprigs fresh thyme
Quarter teaspoon black pepper
Half a beef tomato, sliced
1 large can ackee (approximately
538g)

Ackee with saltfish

1. Soak cod in cold water overnight.
2. Drain in a sieve and refresh under cold running water.
3. Fill a large saucepan with cold water. Add the cod and bring to boil on a high heat.
Simmer for about 20 minutes, drain and rinse under cool water and pat dry on kitchen paper.
4. Flake the fish into smaller pieces and set aside.
5. In a heavy-based pan, heat the oil on medium heat.
6. Add the garlic, sliced onions and scotch bonnet pepper. Allow to cook for a couple of minutes then add the sweet pepper, shallots, black pepper and thyme.
7. Allow this to cook for a further two minutes.
8. Add the pieces of saltfish and cook for another four minutes.
9. Add sliced tomato and warm through for a minute.
10. Stir gently to allow flavours to blend (you may need to add a little extra oil or butter to the pan to stop ingredients from sticking).
11. Open the can of ackee and place in colander to drain (ackee is very fragile so care is needed when handling).
12. Add to frying pan and gently toss with a fork.
13. Serve with rice and a sprinkling of paprika.
14. If you are feeling adventurous, serve with boiled green banana and yellow yam.

 **"Great food, thanks Andy."**
Alex Heywood, Axis Capital

5.

MEAT

450-675g callaloo
2 large knobs of butter
Salt and pepper, to season
Iced water (optional)
1 tablespoon rapeseed oil
4 x 175-225g pieces of kudu (African antelope) loin

For the sauce:
50g shallots, sliced
8 pink peppercorns, crushed
2 juniper berries, crushed
1 bay leaf
4 tablespoons gin
300ml red wine
300ml chicken stock
1 teaspoon plain flour

25g teaspoon butter
1 level tablespoon redcurrant jelly

For the figs:
6 figs, halved lengthwise
2 tablespoons rapeseed oil
25g butter
4 teaspoons demerara sugar
Black pepper

Roast loin of kudu with savoury figs

To make the sauce (this can be prepared beforehand and reheated prior to serving):

1. Place the shallots, peppercorns, juniper berries, bay leaf and gin in a saucepan and bring to the boil. Allow to reduce until almost dry.
2. Add the red wine, return to the boil and reduce in volume by two-thirds.
3. Add the chicken stock and return to the boil, reducing volume by a third.
4. Mix together the flour and butter, then whisk this into the broth.
5. Simmer gently for a few minutes (the mixture will begin to thicken).
6. Whisk in the redcurrant jelly, allowing it to melt into the sauce.
7. Season with a pinch of salt and strain through a fine sieve.

For the callaloo (this can be prepared in advance):

1. Cut leaves and soft stems from the callaloo branches, then soak in a bowl of cold water for about 5-10 minutes.
2. Remove callaloo from water and cut into chunks.
3. In a frying pan, melt a large knob of butter and add callaloo. Stir for about a minute and season to taste. Cover, allowing the callaloo to steam till leaves are tender (approximately 3-4 minutes).
4. Add a tiny bit of water if needed.

Recipe continued overleaf.

Roast loin of kudu with savoury figs (continued)

For the figs:

1. Preheat oven to 200°C/400°F/Gas mark 6.
2. Lightly dust the cut side of each fig with a little flour.
3. Heat the oil in a large frying pan and, once hot, quickly fry the halves, floured-side down, to a golden brown (this should only take a few seconds).
4. Remove the fruit from the pan and place cut side up on a warm baking tray. Dot with the butter and sprinkle with a spoon of demerara sugar and black pepper.
5. Place in the preheated oven for 15-20 minutes, until the figs are tender.

For the kudu loin:

1. Heat the rapeseed oil and remaining butter in a roasting tray on the burner.
2. Once sizzling, season the pieces of meat with salt and pepper and place them in the tray.
3. Fry for a few minutes, until golden brown on all sides.
4. Place the kudu in the preheated oven and roast for eight minutes for a medium-rare finish or 10-12 minutes for medium, turning each piece over halfway through the cooking time.
5. Remove the roasted loins from the oven and leave to rest on a plate for 6-8 minutes.
6. Arrange the callaloo on one side of the plate and place three fig halves side by side on the plate.
7. Pour a spoonful or two of the warmed sauce around the callaloo.
8. Carve the loins into round slices and present them overlapping on top of the callaloo.

If unable to source callaloo, kale can be used as an alternative, although it will have a slightly harder texture.

 *"Fantastic as always."*
James Blackwell, Montpellier

 *"Great lunch."*
Charles Hitchcock, South African pool

Serves 4

40g butter
2 banana shallots, finely chopped
150g mushrooms, finely chopped
150ml sherry
Salt and pepper, to season
4 x 200g veal fillets
2 tablespoons horseradish powder
300g puff pastry
4 slices of Parma ham
1 egg, beaten
1 tablespoon sesame seeds (optional)

2 tablespoons double cream
1 heaped teaspoon of tarragon

For the potatoes:
4 large potatoes (Maris Piper)
150g butter
75ml veal stock
2 sprigs of thyme
2 garlic cloves, crushed
Salt and pepper, to season

For the port sauce:
75g butter
200ml port
450ml chicken stock
Salt and pepper, to season

For the watercress purée:
300g watercress
100g spinach leaves
200ml double cream

Veal wellington in port sauce with watercress purée

For the purée:

1. Put a pan of salted water on to boil. Add the watercress and boil for five minutes.
2. Add the spinach and cook for one minute or so until wilted. Drain in a colander and press with the back of a ladle to remove as much liquid as possible.
3. Put the leaves into a food processor and blend to a fine purée.
4. Pour 60ml cream through the processor funnel and blend till you achieve a sauce with a smooth texture.
5. Add the remaining cream and blend.
6. Season to taste and pour into a small saucepan ready for reheating.

Recipe continued overleaf.

Veal wellington in port sauce with watercress purée (continued)

For the veal:

1. Preheat the oven to 200°C/400°F/Gas mark 6.

2. Melt the butter in a pan and cook the shallots over a low heat until soft, then add the mushrooms and cook until softened.

3. Pour in the sherry together with the cream and tarragon, turn up the heat and cook until the liquid has evaporated.

4. Remove from the heat and season with sea salt and freshly-ground black pepper.

5. Season the veal with horseradish powder.

6. Heat the oil in a pan over a high heat, and then sear the fillets on both sides for 2-3 minutes. Remove and set aside.

7. Roll out the puff pastry thinly and cut out four squares big enough to envelop the meat.

8. Place ham on top of pastry square.

9. Divide the duxelle (mushroom and shallot) mixture between them, leaving enough of a border to seal the pastry.

10. Place a fillet onto each square and brush the edges with the beaten egg. Carefully fold the edges of the pastry to seal the meat inside, then turn over and place on a baking sheet.

11. Brush the tops with the beaten egg. Roll out the remaining pastry and cut squares using a lattice cutter, then carefully place on to each parcel. Brush again with the egg and sprinkle with sesame seeds. Rest in the fridge for 30 minutes before cooking.

12. Cook for 15 minutes for rare and 20 minutes for medium, then set aside to rest.

To make the potatoes:

1. Peel the potatoes and cut into even-sized shapes.

2. Heat the butter in a saucepan over a medium heat. When it starts foaming, add the potatoes and cook for 5-6 minutes on each side.

3. Pour in the stock and add the thyme, crushed garlic, salt and pepper.

4. Cover and reduce the heat so that the stock is simmering.

5. Once cooked through, remove potatoes from the pan and keep warm.

To make the sauce:

1. Melt the butter in the pan used to fry the veal.

2. Add the port and reduce by half. Make up the chicken stock according to the pack instructions, add to the pan and simmer for 2-3 minutes.

3. Season with salt and pepper and serve with the veal wellington, fondant potatoes and watercress purée.

Serves 4

4 lamb shanks
Salt and pepper
3 tablespoons cooking oil
Knob of butter
3 onions, each cut into halves
3 carrots, cut into halves lengthways
1 whole fennel bulb, cut into quarters
3 garlic cloves

Sprig of fresh parsley
Sprig of fresh thyme
1 bay leaf
Juice of 1 orange
50ml Cointreau
Zest of 1 orange
1 bottle red wine
600ml lamb bouillon water
Pinch of brown sugar

For the pumpkin:
1kg pumpkin, skinned and seeded
Knob of butter
1 tablespoon leek, finely chopped
Half teaspoon ground mace
100ml double cream
50-75g Coolea cheese, grated

Lamb shanks with Coolea pumpkin

1. Preheat the oven to 160°C/325°F/Gas mark 3.

2. Season the lamb shanks with salt and pepper. Heat the cooking oil in a large frying pan. When at medium heat, place the shanks in the pan and slowly fry until golden brown (approximately 15-20 minutes). Turn during cooking.

3. Remove from the pan and keep to one side, discarding the fat once cooled.

4. Melt the knob of butter in a braising pot large enough to cook the shanks. Place the onions, carrots, fennel, garlic cloves, parsley, thyme and bay leaf in the pot. Cook over a medium heat for 10-15 minutes until the vegetables are beginning to soften.

5. Add the orange juice, Cointreau, zest, red wine, lamb bouillon and sugar and bring to a simmer. Add the lamb shanks to the pot, cover with a lid and place in the preheated oven. Cook slowly for 2-3 hours, depending on size. Turn and baste the joints, checking their tenderness every 30 minutes.

6. After two hours, check texture. If still firm, cook for a further 30-60 minutes till meat is tender enough to fall off the bone with little to no pressure.

7. Once cooked, carefully lift the shanks from the pot and keep warm to one side. Strain the juice through a sieve.

8. Bring the juice to a simmer, continually skimming away any fat content and impurities. The juice can now be served as thin or thick as you wish. It is important to taste as it simmers and reduces in volume; if too strong, the lamb flavour can be lost behind the overpowering wine reduction.

9. If you feel the flavour is right but a thicker consistency is desired, mix a little water with a teaspoon or two of cornflour and whisk this into the sauce a few drops at a time until the right consistency is achieved. This can then be brushed over the warmed lamb just before serving to give a shiny finish.

10. Return the shanks to the sauce and warm through for 10-15 minutes.

For the pumpkin:

1. Cut the pumpkin into roughly 2.5cm square pieces.

2. Melt the butter in a large saucepan. Once bubbling, add the pumpkin pieces and the leeks. Cook on a medium heat for a few minutes to start the cooking process without colouring. Add four tablespoons of water. Cover with a lid until cooked.

3. Drain off water. Return to heat for a minute to allow water to evaporate – don't colour the pumpkin.

4. Take off heat and add mace, cream and coolea and mash together.

5. Serve with lamb.

Serves 4

For the ox cheeks:
2 ox cheeks, trimmed of fat
3 tablespoons rapeseed oil
250ml red wine
2 tablespoons tomato purée
1 onion, diced
1 carrot, diced

1 celery stalk, diced
Half a small swede, diced
1 small leek, trimmed and diced
1 bacon rasher, sliced
2 sprigs of thyme
1 bay leaf
1 litre beef stock
Salt and pepper, to season

For the dumplings:
100g self-raising flour
50g suet
2 tablespoons horseradish sauce
1 tablespoon flat-leaf parsley, finely
chopped
30g butter

Braised British ox cheeks and horseradish dumplings

1. Preheat the oven to 130°C/250°F/Gas mark ½.
1. Slice each ox cheek into two portions. Heat half of the oil in a pan and sear the cheeks for a couple of minutes on each side until browned.
2. Remove the cheeks and deglaze the pan with the red wine. Boil until the liquid has reduced by half. Stir in the tomato purée.
3. Heat the remaining oil in an ovenproof dish and cook the onions, carrots, celery, swede, leek and bacon for a few minutes, then add the thyme, bay leaf, beef stock and wine mixture. Season with salt and pepper.
4. Add the beef cheeks to the ovenproof dish, cover and cook for three hours (or until the beef is very tender).

For the dumplings:

1. Mix all the ingredients together. Rub the butter into the flour, adding a few spoonfuls of water to bring everything together. Roll into four balls.
2. Add the dumplings to the ox cheeks and cook, uncovered, for a further 25-30 minutes, adding more stock if necessary.
3. To serve, set each ox cheek portion in a bowl, top with a dumpling and serve with seasonal vegetables.

"Nice lunch Andy."
Attila Olah, Hungarian pool

Serves 4

4 x 210g rump of lamb
4 tablespoons olive oil
I fresh thyme sprig
1 sprig rosemary
150g puy lentils
100g butternut squash, diced

100g swede, diced
50g turnip, diced
1 medium leek, washed and diced
3 tablespoons chervil, chopped
5-6 tablespoons reduced balsamic vinegar
Truffle oil

Thyme and rosemary lamb

1. Place lamb in a bowl with half the oil and the thyme and rosemary and leave to marinate.
2. Cook lentils in boiling salted water for 16 minutes. Drain, season and cover to keep hot.
3. Heat the remaining oil in a saucepan, add the vegetables, cover and cook until softened and lightly brown (approximately five minutes).
4. Mix with the lentils and half the chervil. Toss this mixture with a little truffle oil. Cover and set aside.
5. Heat a non-stick frying pan till hot. Add the lamb to the pan and brown for five minutes each side. Lightly season each side as they cook. The lamb should be pink in colour (medium) when ready to be served.
6. Place warm lentils into the centre of the plate.
7. Slice each lamb steak and place on top of lentils.
8. Deglaze the pan with balsamic vinegar and lightly stir for a minute.
9. Spoon juice over lamb, sprinkle with parsley and drizzle the plate with truffle oil.

"True pleasure."
Gary Uricchio, American pool

Serves 1

70g smoked diced pancetta

2-3 tablespoons olive oil

150g chanterelles, cleaned but not washed

1 teaspoon fresh sage, chopped

(optional)

100g baby asparagus

100g samphire

20g pine nuts

Salt and freshly-ground black pepper

Truffle oil

Chanterelles with pancetta and baby asparagus

1. Put a frying pan on a medium heat and cook the pancetta with a couple of tablespoons of oil for four minutes till lightly coloured.

2. Add the chanterelles and keep cooking on a medium heat for four minutes, turning as they cook.

3. Add sage (optional).

4. Stir in the asparagus, samphire and pine nuts and cook for a further minute then remove from heat.

5. Season to taste.

6. Drizzle with truffle oil and serve immediately.

Serves 4

3 whole shallots
125ml red wine
2 cloves garlic, chopped
1 tablespoon olive oil
80g ground allspice
1 teaspoon coarse salt
1 teaspoon minced scotch bonnet pepper
1 teaspoon ground pimento

Half teaspoon ground ginger
450g foie gras, cut into four slices each

For the roasted sweet potato:
680g sweet potato, cut into 2cm cubes
680g puna yam, cut into 2cm cubes
5 tablespoons rapeseed oil
1 plantain

Half teaspoon minced scotch bonnet pepper
475ml coconut milk
2 tablespoons fresh lime juice
1 teaspoon coarse salt
Half teaspoon pink pepper, freshly-ground
Fresh thyme, for garnish

Jamaican jerk foie gras

For the jerk foie gras:

1. In a large bowl, combine all the ingredients except the foie gras.
2. Place the foie gras slices into the seasoning, toss, cover, and refrigerate overnight.

For the roast yam and sweet potato:

1. Preheat the oven to 220˚C/425°F/Gas mark 7.
2. In a small roasting pan, combine the sweet potato, yam and three tablespoons of the rapeseed oil.
3. Roast for approximately 30 minutes until the potato and yam starts to soften. Remove a quarter of the roasted ingredients, reserve, and continue to roast the remaining ingredients for an additional 20 minutes or until slightly caramelised to golden brown.
4. Meanwhile, peel and cut the plantain in half then slice each half into three pieces lengthways.
5. In a frying pan, add remaining oil and heat. Fry plantain gently for 1-2 minutes per side till golden brown. Set aside.
6. In a medium frying pan, add the scotch bonnet and the tablespoon of rapeseed oil together with the reserved potato and yam mixture, coconut milk, lime juice, salt and pepper.
7. Over a medium heat, reduce this mixture by half.
8. Crush the reduced mixture with a potato crusher (or the back of a fork).
9. Set aside both the crushed and the roasted veg mixture and keep warm.

To cook the foie gras:

1. Preheat a grill till very hot.
2. Grill each piece of foie gras for 30 seconds on both sides (medium rare).
3. Spoon a serving of crushed vegetables on to the plate.
4. Place a serving of roasted vegetables on top, then a slice of plantain.
5. Place foie gras to the side.
6. Garnish with a sprig of thyme.

NOTE: For convenience, Walkerswood jerk seasoning can be used.

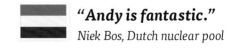

"Andy is fantastic."
Niek Bos, Dutch nuclear pool

Serves 2

2 boneless, skinless guinea fowl thighs, cut into strips
2 boneless, skinless guinea fowl breast, cut into strips
3 tablespoons rapeseed oil

For the marinade:
1 teaspoon sesame oil
2 garlic cloves, peeled and crushed
1 teaspoon chicken stock
2 teaspoons soy sauce
Juice of 1 lime

2 teaspoons ground cumin
1 teaspoon ground coriander
1 large red chilli, trimmed and chopped
2 teaspoons toasted sesame seeds

For the salad:
2 handfuls of mixed salad leaves
2 tablespoons salad dressing of your choice
2 teaspoons toasted sesame seeds
1 tablespoon coriander, chopped
1 lime, halved

Warm guinea fowl salad

1. Place all the ingredients for the marinade except the sesame seeds in a blender and blend until smooth, then stir in the sesame seeds.
2. Put the guinea fowl into a dish, pour over the marinade, cover with clingfilm and marinate in the fridge overnight.
3. Heat a wok over a medium heat for two minutes until almost smoking and add the rapeseed oil.
4. Add the guinea fowl, stirring constantly so the pieces cook evenly. Stir fry for 3-4 minutes until cooked through.
5. Heat a dry frying pan till hot. Add the seeds and shake or stir for about two minutes until they are evenly coloured. Immediately remove from pan.
6. Add salad leaves to dressing.
7. Divide between two plates and scatter over the toasted sesame seeds and chopped coriander.
8. Top with the guinea fowl and serve with lime.

"Wonderful lunch."
William J Nuttall, Letchworth

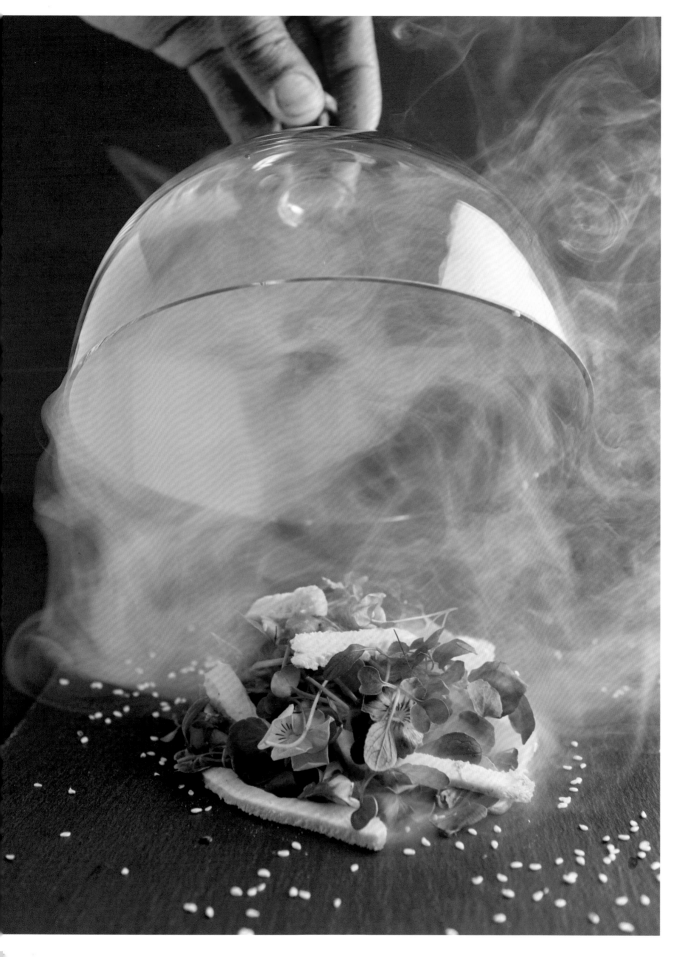

Serves 4
20 large tubular pasta
945ml chicken stock
1 small foie gras
Salt and freshly-ground black pepper

For the truffle sauce:
225ml chicken stock
2 tablespoons butter, chilled
80g goose fat

Pink peppercorns, freshly-ground
Salt
Pinch of smoked paprika
Quarter teaspoon of lemon juice
40g black truffle, chopped
1 tablespoon truffle juice

For the ricotta sauce:
Knob of butter
1 chilli, finely chopped

115ml thick, heavy double cream
Pinch of smoked paprika
Fine sea salt
Cornflour, to thicken
50g ricotta cheese

For the garnish:
10g black truffle, finely sliced

Foie gras-filled pasta with two sauces

For the pasta:

1. Cook the pasta in the chicken stock till al dente (approximately six minutes).

2. Remove from the chicken stock and refresh in an ice bath for a few seconds. Drain and dry pasta.

3. Bring the stock back up to a boil and poach the foie gras on a low simmer heat for five minutes. Remove and drain.

4. Cut the foie gras into 20 pieces, making sure each piece will fit inside the pasta. Season the foie gras with salt and black pepper. Fill each piece of pasta with a piece of foie gras and put to one side.

For the truffle sauce:

1. In a saucepan reduce the chicken stock by half over a low heat. Whisk a tablespoon of butter and goose fat to form an emulsion. Add peppercorns, smoked paprika and lemon juice, strain through a fine sieve and set to one side.

2. Over a low heat, melt the remaining tablespoon of butter in a small pan. Add the chopped truffle and cook slowly for four minutes. Pour in the truffle juice and reduce the mixture by half.

3. Combine this truffle mixture with the reserved sauce.

For the ricotta sauce:

1. In a saucepan melt the butter, add chilli and gently warm for 30 seconds. Add cream, paprika and salt. Thicken with cornflour and remove from heat. Stir in the ricotta and set aside.

To serve:

1. Arrange the stuffed pasta in the basket of a steamer in a single layer and set over simmering water. Steam for three minutes or until the pasta and foie gras are warmed through.

2. Place five stuffed pasta tubes on each of the serving plates.

3. Top with the truffle sauce then drizzle with the ricotta sauce.

4. Garnish with sliced truffle.

"Excellent tasty food."
Gilles Trembley, French pool

Serves 4

For the potato cake:
5 large potatoes, peeled and quartered
150g Parmesan, finely-grated
1 pinch nutmeg or mace
3 teaspoons pink peppercorns,
crushed
1 teaspoon Maldon salt

For the venison:
4 x 220g venison fillet
Salt and freshly-ground pepper

For the fruity sauce:
Zest of 1 lime, 1 orange and 1 lemon
Juice of half lemon and half
grapefruit
80ml honey
3 juniper berries
2 star anise
750ml chicken stock
100ml red wine
1 sprig rosemary
1 sprig thyme

For the vegetables:
Knob of butter
Squeeze of lemon juice
225g French fine beans
30g dried cranberries
Salt and pepper, to taste
55g pomegranate seeds

To serve:
Dried onions
Smoked bacon

Venison and potato cake with a fruity sauce

For the potato cake:

1. Boil the potatoes in salted water. When soft, drain and put back on the heat to make sure all the water has evaporated.
2. Cool, add the rest of the ingredients and mix well. Shape into four cakes.

For the venison:

1. Season the venison and sear in a very hot frying pan.
2. Bake in the oven at 180°C/350°F/Gas mark 4 for 5-10 minutes (five minutes rare and ten minutes medium).
3. Stand for five minutes before serving.

For the fruity sauce:

1. Combine the zests, juices, honey, juniper berries and star anise and caramelise.
2. Add the rest of the ingredients and reduce by half or until the sauce thickens.

For the vegetables:

1. Melt the butter with the lemon juice. Fry the green beans and cranberries until al dente.
2. Add salt and pepper to taste.
3. Remove from heat then add the pomegranate seeds and toss together.

To serve:

1. Pour a little sauce into the middle of the plate and place the potato cake on top.
2. Place the meat on top of the cake and then add the French beans, cranberries and pomegranate.
3. Garnish with dried onions and crispy smoked bacon.

For the artichoke mash:
5 large potatoes, peeled and diced
5 small Jerusalem artichokes, peeled and diced
60g butter
1 large onion, finely chopped
2 carrots, peeled and finely chopped
2 sticks celery, finely chopped
1 leek, finely chopped
3 garlic cloves, finely chopped

1 teaspoon sage
Oil, for frying
1 tablespoon lemon juice
2 tablespoons lime juice
Half glass madeira
Half glass port
300ml red wine
500ml vegetable stock
1 heaped teaspoon tarragon
4 portobello mushrooms
4 king oyster mushrooms

For the bison steak:
60ml cup extra virgin olive oil
125ml sherry vinegar
1 teaspoon sea salt
1 clove garlic, chopped
1 teaspoon freshly-ground black pepper
Small piece stem ginger, chopped
4 x 190g bison fillets

Bison steak with artichoke mash and mushrooms

1. Boil the potatoes and artichokes in salted water. When soft, drain and put back on the heat to make sure all the water has evaporated. Mash with a little butter and set aside.
2. Fry the onions, carrots, celery, leeks, garlic and sage in a little butter and olive oil till vegetables are lightly caramelised.
3. Add both lemon and lime juice and reduce till almost dry.
4. Add madeira and port and reduce again.
5. Stir in wine and stock, then simmer until reduced by half.
6. Strain gravy and then add tarragon (put aside solid bits).
7. Return gravy to pan and add mushrooms, gill side up. Season.
8. Simmer gently for 10-15 minutes until sauce is rich and reduced in quantity. Set aside.

For the bison steak:
1. Combine olive oil, vinegar, salt, garlic, cracked black pepper and stem ginger. Toss with steaks and coat well.
2. Marinate overnight in the refrigerator.
3. Grill for four minutes on each side, taking care not to overcook the steak.
4. Remove from the grill and rest for two minutes.
5. Position on top of mushrooms.

Serves 2

For the potatoes:
150g butter
4 potatoes, peeled and cut into your
desired shape
75ml vegetable stock
1 garlic clove, peeled and crushed
3 sprigs fresh thyme
Sea salt and pepper, to taste

For the liver:
60ml rapeseed oil
250g red onions, sliced
150g yellow peppers, seeded and cut
into slices
400g calf's liver, cut into thin slices
25g salt
5g black pepper, freshly-ground
2g sage
10g paprika

Calf's liver

For the potatoes:

1. Heat the butter over a medium heat in a saucepan. When the butter is foaming, add the potatoes and fry until deep golden-brown on one side (approximately five minutes).
2. Turn over the potatoes and cook other side until golden brown.
3. Carefully pour in the stock, then add the garlic cloves and thyme sprigs and season to taste, with salt and freshly-ground black pepper.
4. Cover the pan with a lid and reduce the heat until the stock is simmering. Simmer the potatoes until tender, then remove from the pan and keep warm.

For the liver:

1. Fry the onions lightly in the oil till just golden brown.
2. Add the peppers and liver.
3. Whilst stirring, season with salt, pepper and sage. Sauté over high heat, adding paprika to taste. The liver should remain pink in colour.
4. Serve with seasonal vegetables.

"Very tasty Andy."
Danilo Antoncic, Slovenian pool

"Brilliant."
Sean Granville, New Brunswick Power

Serves 4

For the beans:
200g dried cannellini beans, soaked in water overnight
1 onion, halved
1 clove garlic, split
2 sprigs thyme
100ml double cream
1 teaspoon chopped chives

3 teaspoons wholegrain mustard

For the fennel:
2 tablespoons olive oil
1 clove garlic, halved
2 medium fennel bulbs
Half a carrot
A few slices of leek
75ml white wine

200ml chicken stock

For the pork:
4 x 150g pork loin fillet
Salt and green peppercorns
100ml olive oil
25g butter
1 sprig thyme
1 garlic clove, crushed

For the black pudding:
4 slices black pudding
1 tablespoon rapeseed oil

For the stock:
50ml chicken stock
10ml red wine
50g butter

Pork loin with black pudding

For the beans:
1. Make the beans first. Drain soaked beans and transfer to a large pot. Cover with cold water, add onion, garlic and thyme and bring to a boil. Skim off and discard any foam on the surface.
2. Reduce heat, cover and simmer, gently stirring occasionally, until beans are tender (1 to 1.5 hours).
3. Drain beans and discard onions, garlic and thyme.
4. Add double cream, chives and mustard. Reduce on a low heat. Set aside and keep warm.

For the fennel:
1. While the beans are cooking, make the braised fennel. In a pan, heat olive oil and fry garlic until golden brown. Add fennel, carrot and leek. Sauté for a few minutes.
2. Pour in wine and stock and reduce heat to simmer. Cook for 25-30 minutes until fennel is tender. Set aside and keep warm.

For the pork loin:
1. Season pork fillet with salt. Add olive oil to a heavy-based frying pan and seal the pork fillet over a moderate heat. Continue to brown the meat, turning regularly, for approximately six minutes.
2. Place the pork in the oven still in its hot pan and cook for five minutes at 180°C/350°F/Gas mark 4, turning once halfway through cooking. Ensure you do not overcook as the fillet should be succulent.
3. Remove pan from the oven and add the butter, thyme and garlic. Allow this to bubble and foam as you baste both sides of the fillet. When you feel the meat is ready, remove from pan and keep warm.

For the black pudding:
1. Heat the oil in a shallow frying pan. Cook the black pudding for 3-4 minutes on each side. Remove from pan.

For the stock:
1. Put all ingredients in frying pan and reduce by half.

To serve:
1. Place fennel in the centre of a warm plate, put black pudding on top followed by pork to create a stack. Place beans in a circle around the meat and mask with stock.

For the red cabbage coleslaw:
1 small red cabbage, leaves shredded
2 carrots, peeled and grated
Half a red onion, peeled and very thinly sliced
Half a white onion, peeled and very thinly sliced
250ml malt vinegar
Salt

400ml good quality mayonnaise
2 tablespoons wholegrain mustard

For the potato wedges:
4 large potatoes, cut into wedges
2 tablespoons olive oil
Freshly-ground black pepper
1 sprig fresh thyme, leaves only
2 garlic cloves, unpeeled
1 sprig fresh rosemary, leaves only

Salt, to taste

For the ostrich burgers:
2 red onions
4 ostrich burgers (these are obtainable from the Exotic Meat Company)
4 ciabatta rolls, halved
1 beef tomato

Ostrich burger with potato wedges and red cabbage coleslaw

For the red cabbage coleslaw (preferably make this the day before):
1. Combine the cabbage, carrots and onions in a large serving bowl. Add malt vinegar and season with salt. Stir in the mayonnaise and the mustard. Add seasoning to taste.
2. Refrigerate.

For the potato wedges:
1. Preheat the oven to 220°C/425°F/Gas mark 7.
2. Bring a pot of salted water to the boil. Carefully drop the wedges into the pan and boil for four minutes, then drain well.
3. Put the potato wedges in a bowl and drizzle with olive oil. Add pepper, thyme, garlic and rosemary. Sprinkle with salt.
4. Place on a baking tray and roast for 30 minutes, or until golden brown and tender.

For the ostrich burgers:
1. Meanwhile heat a frying pan until hot and fry the onion. When lightly coloured, remove from the pan and set aside in a warm place. Using the same pan, fry the burgers for 3-4 minutes on each side until cooked, then set aside.
2. Preheat the grill and toast the ciabatta until crisp. Lightly grill the tomatoes.
3. Put the burger on the toasted ciabatta and top with tomato and onion. Serve with the potato wedges and red cabbage coleslaw.

"Gorgeous food."
Emma Sangeelee, Edwin Coe LLP

Serves 4

For the sweet potato terrine:
1kg sweet potatoes
Salt and pepper
200g butter, melted

For the marinade:
Quarter teaspoon each of garlic
powder, smoked paprika and soy sauce
Black pepper

Salt
1 green chilli
2 sprigs rosemary
1 clove garlic
2 tablespoons rapeseed oil

For the partridge:
2 tablespoons olive oil
2 garlic cloves, chopped
4 partridges

Small glass of white wine
250ml chicken stock
Salt and pepper

For the sprouts:
400g shredded sprouts
Knob of butter
8 baby carrots, sliced lengthways
2 spring onions
10g pine nuts

Roast partridge with black garlic and sweet potato terrine

For the sweet potato terrine (make this first):

1. Preheat the oven to 160°C/325°F/Gas mark 3.
2. Smear the bottom and sides of a terrine mould with butter.
3. Peel the potatoes and slice into thin rounds.
4. Season and pour over the melted butter. Mix thoroughly.
5. Carefully layer the potatoes to the top of the terrine mould.
6. Cover with kitchen foil, set in a bain-marie (water bath) and bake for approximately one hour, until the potatoes are tender.
7. Turn out of the mould, slice and serve.

For the partridge:

1. Combine the marinade ingredients in a bowl and mix together. Spoon over the partridge and place in fridge overnight.
2. Heat two tablespoons of olive oil in a large frying pan, add the garlic then brown the partridges on all sides.
3. Place in a roasting tin. Roast for approximately 20-25 minutes.
4. Remove the partridges, deglaze the pan with the white wine and reduce the liquid by half. Add the chicken stock, simmer for ten minutes and season to taste. Keep warm.

For the buttered sprouts:

1. Blanch the sprouts in salted, boiling water for one minute until tender. Drain.
2. Melt a knob of butter in a large frying pan and add the sliced carrots and spring onions. Sauté until softened.
3. Add the sprouts, sauté for a further minute then sprinkle on the pine nuts and serve.

"Great lunch, thank you."
Milos Posad, Czech Republic pool

Serves 6

For the marinade:
2 tablespoons white wine
Half teaspoon each of smoked garlic
(finely chopped) and salt
2 teaspoons wholegrain mustard
Level teaspoon each of dried thyme
and ground coriander
Pinch of ground cumin
2 tablespoons olive oil

1 teaspoon sage
White pepper

For the mushroom filling:
2 tablespoons olive oil
150g mushrooms of choice, cleaned
and sliced
1 leek, finely chopped
1 clove of garlic, minced
1 tablespoon parsley, chopped

Salt and pepper

For the quail:
6 quails, semi-boneless
1 tablespoon vegetable oil
500ml chicken stock

Roast quail with leeks, red onion and mushroom

1. Preheat the oven to 180°C/350°F/Gas mark 4.
2. Combine all the marinade ingredients and store them in the fridge until they are needed.
3. For the mushroom filling, heat the olive oil over a medium heat in a sauté pan.
4. Stir in the mushrooms, onion and leeks and cook until soft.
5. Stir in the garlic, parsley, salt and pepper to taste.
6. Set aside to cool – ideally overnight.
7. Remove the wing tip from the quails and brush with the marinade.
8. Place in a bowl, refrigerate and leave to marinate.
9. Stuff each quail with the cold mushroom filling and refrigerate until ready to cook.
10. In a non-stick sauté pan heat one tablespoon of vegetable oil. Add the quail and lightly brown.
11. Place in the oven and roast for 10-15 minutes until cooked as desired. Season and place on serving plate.
12. Drain any remaining juice from the pan, deglaze with stock and reduce.
13. Season with salt to taste and pour the sauce over the quails. Serve with seasonal vegetables or crisp salad.

"Splendid. Good food."
Mark Armitage, Cumbria

"Fantastic, thanks chef."
Charles Hitchcock, South African pool

Serves 4
4g peppercorns (white, green, black and pink)
2 sprigs of thyme
Pinch of salt
4 x 210g fillet steaks
140g fresh foie gras, sliced into four pieces, lightly scored and seasoned
Vegetable oil and butter, for frying

Brioche, to serve
Black truffle oil, to garnish

For the sauce:
350ml port
700ml chicken stock
700ml veal stock
200g unsalted butter

Peppered fillet steak

For the steaks:

1. Grind the peppercorns with thyme to a medium/coarse consistency and add a pinch of salt.
2. Rub each steak in the mixture.
3. Set aside and refrigerate, preferably overnight or for at least four hours.

For the sauce:

1. Reduce 250ml of the port by three quarters, until syrup-like in consistency.
2. Add chicken and veal stock and simmer, uncovered until reduced by half.
3. Add the rest of the port, boil the sauce rapidly and whisk in the chilled butter. Simmer, stirring constantly, until you have a glossy sauce.

To serve:

1. Heat a frying pan with a little oil and butter. Fry the steaks for 3-4 minutes on each side (5-6 minutes for well done), basting the meat with the butter.
2. Remove from the pan and keep warm.
3. In another very hot pan, fry the foie gras until browned (approximately one minute each side).
4. Garnish with black truffle oil and serve with a slice of toasted brioche and vegetables of your choice.

 **"The beef was fantastic."**
Joe Aldous, RGL Forensics

 **"Great lunch Andy."**
Ben Shaw, Benjamin Shaw Events

Serves 4

For the potato and pancetta terrine:
1kg potatoes
180g butter, melted
8 rashers smoked streaky bacon
Salt and pepper

For the pheasant:
80g toasted macadamia nuts
115g salted butter

1 teaspoon chervil
1 clove black garlic, smoked and peeled
4 large pheasant breasts
Salt and pepper, to season
25g plain flour, seasoned with salt and pepper
2 eggs, beaten
50g breadcrumbs
1 tablespoon olive oil

Pheasant kiev with pancetta stack

For the potato and pancetta terrine (make this first):

1. Preheat the oven to 160°C/325°F/Gas mark 3.
2. Rub the inside of a terrine mould with butter.
3. Peel the potatoes and slice into thin rounds.
4. Season and pour over the melted butter. Mix thoroughly.
5. Layer the potatoes to the top of the terrine mould, placing the bacon strips evenly in alternative layers.
6. Cover with kitchen foil, set in a bain-marie and bake for about 1-1.5 hours, until the potatoes are tender.
7. Turn out of the mould, slice and serve.

For the pheasant:

1. Preheat the oven to 180°C/350°F/Gas mark 4.
2. To make the garlic butter, place the macadamia nuts, 50g of the butter, chervil and the clove of garlic in a food processor and blend. Set aside.
3. Take the pheasant breasts and make small incisions into the underside. Fill these with the garlic butter, season well with salt and freshly-ground black pepper. Then place the mini fillet over the top of the incision to seal.
4. Carefully pass the pheasant kiev through the seasoned flour, then the eggs and finally the breadcrumbs.
5. Heat the oil in an ovenproof frying pan. Gently fry the kiev until lightly coloured on one side then transfer to the oven for 12-15 minutes.
6. Serve with the terrine and seasonal vegetables.

"An excellent dinner."
Pavel Rudenskiy, Russian pool

Serves 4

For the marinade:
400ml good-quality red wine
1 tablespoon redcurrant jelly
1 small onion, chopped
1 stick celery, chopped
1 large carrot, chopped
1 smoked garlic clove, crushed
1 sprig fresh rosemary
1 bay leaf
1 small leek, chopped
1 sprig fresh parsley
4 peppercorns, cracked

For the casserole:
4 medium-sized chicken breasts
3 tablespoons seasoned plain flour
2 tablespoons olive oil, plus extra for frying
100g smoked pancetta
20 button onions, peeled
20 button mushrooms
1 tablespoon cognac
Salt and black pepper, to season
Olive oil, for shallow frying
4 slices thick brown bread, crusts removed

Chicken with red wine sauce

1. Place the marinade ingredients into a small pot and bring to the boil until reduced by a third. Pass through a fine sieve into a bowl and leave to cool.
2. Place the chicken into the marinade, cover and leave to chill in the fridge overnight.
3. Remove the chicken from the marinade and reserve the liquid.
4. Season with salt and freshly-ground black pepper.
5. Dip the chicken in the seasoned flour and fry until golden brown in a little olive oil. Remove and set aside.
6. Warm the olive oil in a frying pan and gently fry the pancetta until golden brown.
Add the onions and mushrooms and fry gently until golden brown. Remove any excess fat and return the chicken to the pot. Turn up the heat and pour over the cognac. Flambé and allow the flames to die down before adding the reserved marinade.
7. Gently simmer for approximately 30 minutes (meat should be soft to the touch with a fork).
8. Heat a small amount of vegetable oil in a heavy-based frying pan. Pan-fry the bread until golden brown.
9. Serve the chicken breast with wild rice and bread.

"Wonderful chicken."
Alain Quere, Swiss pool

Serves 4

For the marinade:

2 teaspoons salt

1 teaspoon black pepper

5-6 tablespoons curry powder

1 large onion, sliced

4-6 cloves garlic, minced

1 scotch bonnet pepper, sliced and deseeded

For the goat:

1.5kg goat meat, diced

4 tablespoons cooking oil

1 large sprig thyme

945ml boiling water

1 medium onion, chopped

Curried goat

1. Mix all marinade ingredients together in a bowl. Spoon over the meat, cover and place in the fridge overnight.

2. Remove the sliced onions and scotch bonnet pepper from the bowl of marinated meat and set aside.

3. Heat cooking oil in heavy-based pan.

4. Place goat meat in pan and brown.

5. Add the thyme and half of the boiling water. Cover, lower heat and simmer for about one hour (ensure this does not boil dry).

6. Chop one medium onion and add to pot along with the sliced onion and scotch bonnet pepper that was set aside earlier.

7. Add the remaining boiling water and bring to a boil.

8. Taste and remove scotch bonnet pepper if desired flavour has been reached. At this stage you can add additional curry powder if desired.

9. Simmer on low heat for 30 minutes or until the meat is falling off the bone.

10. Serve with rice and a crisp green salad.

"Superb as always."
Keith Wise, London

6.

DESSERTS

Serves 4

For the chocolate sponge:
25g cocoa powder
1 teaspoon cinnamon
100g flour
4 eggs
120g sugar
1 teaspoon brandy

25g melted butter at room temperature

For the cherry sauce:
2 tablespoons cornflour
410g black cherries in juice
1 tablespoon caster sugar
3 tablespoons kirsch

For the syrup:
100ml sugar
100ml water
3 tablespoons kirsch

For the cream:
1 fresh vanilla pod
30g caster sugar

300ml whipping cream
1 teaspoon ground cinnamon

To garnish:
8 fresh cherries

Cherry and chocolate cake in a glass

For the chocolate sponge:

1. Preheat the oven to 170°C/325°F/Gas mark 3 and line a 15cm round cake tin.
2. Add cocoa and cinnamon to flour, combine and sift.
3. Whisk the eggs, sugar and brandy until they form a thick cream-like consistency. Fold the flour into the cream mixture, adding the butter when halfway through the process. Continue mixing until the mixture is smooth.
4. Pour the batter into the tin. Bake for approximately 20 minutes (check centre to ensure cake is cooked). Place on rack to cool.
5. When cool, cut the cake into cubes and set aside (this can be made in advance).

For the cherry sauce:

1. Place the cornflour in a small bowl, add three tablespoons of the cherry juice and mix into a paste.
2. Heat the rest of the cherry juice with the sugar. When boiling, whisk in the cornflour solution off the heat, then return to the boil for a minute or so until thickened.
3. Stir in the cherries then pour the whole mixture into a bowl. Add the kirsch and leave to cool.

For the syrup:

1. Bring the sugar and water to the boil and remove from the heat once the sugar is dissolved. When cooled, add the kirsch to taste.

For the cream:

1. Scrape the seeds from half of the vanilla pod and add to sugar, cream and cinnamon.
2. Whisk to form soft peaks.
3. Place in fridge.

To serve:

1. Place a layer of chocolate sponge in the bottom of four glasses (or a large bowl).
2. Spoon over a little kirsch syrup to moisten the sponge. Top with a layer of cherry sauce then spoon the cream on top. Decorate with fresh cherries and serve.

 "A very enjoyable experience, as ever."
Janet Copping, Price Forbes

Serves 4

For the sponge:
3 large eggs
90g caster sugar
90g plain flour, sifted
50g unsalted butter, melted and
cooled

For the syrup:
100g caster sugar
125ml water
1 strip of lemon

Sherry, to taste
Squeeze of lemon juice

For the custard:
200ml milk
100ml whipping cream
1 fresh vanilla pod, split
75g caster sugar
4 egg yolks
1 teaspoon ground cinnamon
25g custard powder

For the raspberry mixture:
8 tablespoons raspberry jam
125g fresh raspberries, plus a few for
decoration

For the cream:
500ml whipping cream
75g caster sugar
Seeds scraped from half a vanilla pod

To garnish:
Toppings of your choice

Trifle

For the sponge:
1. Preheat the oven to 180°C/350°F/Gas mark 4.
2. Whisk the eggs and sugar and in a large bowl, until you have a thick cream-like consistency which will hold its shape. Fold in the flour and melted butter.
3. Pour the mixture into a thin baking tin which has been greased and lined with baking parchment. Bake for 10-12 minutes or until it springs back when pressed lightly at the centre. Turn the sponge out and cool on a wire rack to cool.

For the syrup:
1. Bring the sugar, water and strip of lemon to the boil and remove from the heat once the sugar has dissolved.
2. Cool the syrup and then add the sherry and lemon juice.

For the custard:
1. Bring the milk, cream and vanilla to the boil.
2. Whisk the sugar, egg yolks, cinnamon and custard powder together.
3. Whisk the boiling milk mixture onto the yolks mixture, and return to the pan. Cook over a moderate heat, stirring at all times until the mixture has bubbled for about a minute. Pass the mixture through a fine sieve, cover with clingfilm and keep warm.

For the raspberry mixture:
1. Place the jam and raspberries in a bowl and combine with a fork, crushing the raspberries a little as you go.

To serve:
1. Cut the cooled sponge into 2cm squares, and place a layer into the base of the glass. Spoon over enough syrup to moisten the sponge.
2. Top the sponge with a layer of raspberry mixture, followed by a layer of warm custard. Allow the custard layer to cool completely in the fridge.
3. Meanwhile, whip the cream with the caster sugar and vanilla to give a soft peak consistency. When the custard layer is chilled, spoon the vanilla cream on the top to fill the glasses. Decorate with the topping of your choice.

Makes 20
110g butter
2 tablespoons sugar
2 tablespoons golden syrup
4 teaspoons good quality cocoa
225g digestive biscuits, crushed
1 handful dried cranberries
225g Callebaut cooking chocolate –
half milk and half dark

Chocolate tiffin

1. In a saucepan, melt the butter, sugar, syrup and cocoa.
2. Stir the biscuits and cranberries into the mixture.
3. Pour the mixture into a Swiss roll-size tin and press down.
4. Melt the chocolate and pour over the mixture in the tin.
5. Pop the tin into the fridge and leave to set (approximately an hour).
6. Cut into about 20 pieces and serve.

"Great chocolates."
Phil Chamberlain, Willis

Makes 20

175g icing sugar
125g finely ground almonds
3 large free-range egg whites
Pinch of salt
75g caster sugar

2 food colourings and flavours of choice
Nuts of your choice (optional)

For the filling:
150g butter, softened
75g icing sugar

Multicoloured macaroons

1. Preheat the oven to 160°C/325°F/Gas mark 3.
2. Line two baking trays with parchment or baking paper and set aside.
3. Blend icing sugar and ground almonds in a food processor to a very fine mixture. Sift into a bowl.
4. In a separate bowl, whisk the egg whites with a pinch of salt to soft peaks.
5. Gradually whisk in the caster sugar until thick and glossy. Divide this mixture between two bowls.
6. Add food flavouring and colour of your choice to each bowl.
7. Divide the almond and icing sugar mixture into two. Fold half of each mixture into the meringue and mix well. Add the remaining half, making sure you use a spatula to cut and fold the mixture until it is shiny and thick.
8. Spoon into a piping bag fitted with a 1cm plain nozzle (this step will need to be undertaken twice). Pipe small rounds of the macaroon mixture, about 3cm across, onto the baking sheets. Leave to stand at room temperature for 10-15 minutes to form a slight skin. At this stage you should be able to touch them lightly without any mixture sticking to your finger.
9. Bake for 15 minutes.
10. Remove from the oven and cool.
11. Meanwhile, in a bowl beat the butter until light and fluffy, then beat in the icing sugar.
12. Add colour, flavouring or nuts. Use this mixture to fill the macaroons.

"Great lunch."
Danny Clack, Pembroke

Makes 4

For the crusts:
190g plain flour
32g sugar
Pinch of salt
140g cold unsalted butter,
cut into small pieces
1 egg yolk

2 tablespoons cold water
Quarter teaspoon vanilla
extract

For the filling:
210g sugar
2 tablespoons finely-grated
lemon zest
100ml fresh lemon juice

80ml fresh orange juice
2 tablespoons cornstarch
60ml water
1 large egg, plus 3 egg yolks
6 tablespoons unsalted
butter, cut into pieces
3 tablespoons lemon-
flavoured liqueur

For the meringue:
3 large egg whites
Half teaspoon cream of
tartar
7 tablespoons sugar

Lemon meringue tartlets

To make the crusts:

1. Pulse the flour, sugar and salt in a food processor. Add the cold butter and pulse till the mixture resembles large breadcrumbs.

2. In a bowl combine the egg yolk, ice water and vanilla and stir well. Add to the food processor and pulse to combine. Shape the dough into a ball, wrap it with clingfilm and refrigerate for a couple of hours.

3. Preheat an oven to 180°C/350°F/Gas mark 4.

4. Divide the dough into four parts and roll each into a ball. Butter four 4-inch tins (preferably with removable bottoms), and place the dough into the tins, pressing into bottom and up the sides. Place in freezer for about ten minutes.

5. Prick the bottom of each tart with a fork. Bake the shells for between 20-25 minutes until golden brown.

6. Remove the tartlets from the oven and let them cool completely.

For the filling:

1. Whisk the sugar, lemon zest, lemon juice, orange juice, cornstarch and 60ml water in a medium saucepan until smooth.

2. Whisk in the whole egg and egg yolks.

3. Cook over a medium heat, whisking, until the mixture simmers (about five minutes).

4. Add the butter and liqueur and continue whisking over medium heat until the mixture thickens.

5. Spoon the curd into the prepared crusts.

For the meringue:

1. Beat the egg whites in a medium bowl until they look like foam.

2. Sprinkle in the cream of tartar and continue beating until soft peaks appear. Gradually beat in the sugar until the mixture resembles stiff shiny peaks.

3. Transfer the meringue to a pastry bag fitted with a star tip and pipe onto the tarts.

4. Bake for approximately 15 minutes or till the meringue is set and golden.

5. Let them cool completely before removing from the tins.

 "Great meal."
Oleksandr Babenko, Ukrainian pool

Makes 18 cakes

750ml milk
1 level teaspoon vanilla extract
210g unsalted butter
200g light brown sugar

150g plain flour
2 eggs, plus 1 egg yolk
3 tablespoons Jamaican white rum
30g butter, for greasing
Icing sugar, for sprinkling

Rum and vanilla canelés

1. In a saucepan, place the milk and vanilla extract. Bring to a boil.
2. Once boiled, remove the pan from the heat and add the three tablespoons of butter. Set aside to cool to lukewarm.
3. In a large bowl, mix together the sugar and flour.
4. In a separate bowl, whisk together the eggs, egg yolk and rum.
5. Whisk the egg mixture into the sugar and flour mixture, then whisk in the lukewarm milk mixture till the liquid is smooth and resembles batter.
6. Cover and refrigerate overnight (this can then be kept for between 12 and 48 hours, so can be done in advance).
7. Remove the batter from the fridge at least an hour before baking.
8. Preheat the oven to 220°C/425°F/Gas mark 7.
9. Liberally butter the inside of 18 canelé moulds then sprinkle sugar into the moulds.
10. Place the moulds on a baking tray or sheet. Fill them three-quarters full with the batter. Ensure the sugar and batter remain evenly distributed.
11. Bake till a brown crust appears on top (the cake should still be moist inside). This can take between 50-70 minutes.
12. Remove from the oven.
13. Gently remove cake from mould, set aside to cool then serve.

"Excellent meal, thanks."
Colin Stobbart, Rolls Royce

6 medium free-range eggs, whites
only
330g caster sugar
1 tablespoon cacao powder
2 tablespoon conserve (raspberry,
mango, strawberry etc, to reflect your
preferred taste)

Giant meringues

1. Preheat oven to 110°C/230°F/gas mark ¼.
2. Line two baking sheets with greaseproof paper.
3. In a bowl, whisk the egg whites until they form stiff peaks then slowly add the caster sugar a small amount at a time, whisking to ensure it is combined.
4. Divide the mixture between two bowls (if making different flavours), then gently fold the cacao powder into one and the conserve into the other.
5. Using a large spoon, drop oval shaped meringues on a baking tray.
6. Bake in the oven for two hours, then turn the oven off and leave in the warm oven for a further hour before removing.
7. Allow to cool before serving.

Makes 6

100g Callebaut dark chocolate
100g butter
2 eggs
70g caster sugar
50g flour
1 teaspoon cinnamon
10g cocoa or cacao
1 teaspoon baking powder

Chocolate fondant

1. Butter six ramekins, ensuring the surface is completely covered. Set aside.
2. Half fill a saucepan with water and bring to a gentle simmer.
3. Place a bowl with the chocolate and butter inside on top of the pan and slowly melt.
4. Remove from the heat and mix well together.
5. Whisk together the eggs and sugar. Once the mixture is pale, creamy and fluffy, fold into the chocolate.
6. Add the flour, cinnamon, cocoa and baking powder and continue to fold until nice and even. Divide the mixture between the ramekins and chill for around an hour – this can be made the night before .
7. When ready to cook, preheat the oven to 200°C/400°F/Gas mark 6.
8. Cook for 8-10 minutes until the tops have formed a crust. Remove from oven.
9. These can now be served warm, or gently removed from the ramekins and served on a plate with the accompaniment of your choice.

"Absolutely fantastic."
JacquesPlourde, Canadian pool

Serves 6
200g butter
200g caster sugar, plus
additional 6 tablespoons
3 eggs
200g ground almonds
100g fine cornmeal
1 teaspoon baking powder
2 lemons
1 lime

Lemon cake

1. Preheat the oven to 180°C/350°F/Gas mark 4.

2. Grease and line an 8-inch round cake tin.

3. In a bowl, beat the butter and sugar until light and fluffy. Add in the eggs one by one and beat well, adding in a small amount of ground almonds if mixture starts to curdle.

4. Add in the remaining ground almonds and again beat well.

5. Stir in the cornmeal and baking powder.

6. Grate in the zest of one of the lemons and the juice of half a lime.

7. Mix well and place the mixture into your prepared tin.

8. Bake in the middle of the oven for between 45 minutes and an hour (check cake with a skewer).

9. While the cake is cooking, grate the rind off the lime and extract the juice from the remaining lemons and lime.

10. Place the rind and the juice in a small saucepan with the six tablespoons of sugar. Stir to combine and then heat over a gentle heat until the sugar has dissolved.

11. When the cake is cooked, remove it from the oven and prick all over with a skewer – immediately pour the lemon syrup over the cake and let it soak in.

12. Leave to cool, then remove and wrap in foil until needed.

13. Serve.

"Fantastic food."
Kathryn Brown, London

Serves 2
1 medium-sized sweet pineapple
16 whole cloves
250g caster sugar
460ml water
1 teaspoon Chinese five-spice powder

1 cinnamon stick
1 star anise
1 stem ginger bulb
2 teaspoons nutmeg
1 small red whole chilli

Baby roasted pineapple

1. Cut off the top of the pineapple, peel and remove the 'eyes' then slice.
2. Push the cloves into the 'eye sockets'.
3. To make the syrup sauce, place the sugar and four tablespoons of water in a heavy-based saucepan and dissolve very slowly over a low heat. Try not to stir.
4. Once syrup is clear and no sugar grains remain, increase the heat and continue to boil for about 6-8 minutes to achieve a light caramel colour.
5. Remove from the heat and slowly stir in 400ml water, followed by the spices.
6. Place the pineapple in a large heavy-based pan and pour over the caramel syrup.
7. Heat gently for about five minutes, basting with the syrup.
8. Transfer the pineapple to a bowl, pour over the syrup and set aside to cool. Cover and leave to soften overnight.
9. When ready to cook, preheat oven to 190°C/375°F/Gas mark 5. Place the pineapple in a roasting tin and spoon over some of the syrup. Roast for 15-20 minutes, basting two or three times with the syrup.
10. The pineapple should now be left to cool to room temperature.
11. Serve the pineapple with some of the spiced syrup spooned over.

"Excellent meal."
John TeBogt, Marsh

Serves 4
125g butter
225g plain flour
225g sugar, plus 2 tablespoons for
dusting the top of the cobbler
1 teaspoon baking powder
170ml whole milk
6 large peaches, sliced
Cream and blackberries to serve

Peach cobbler

1. Preheat the oven to 150°C/300°F/Gas mark 2.
2. Melt the butter in a baking dish.
3. Mix the flour, sugar, baking powder and milk together.
4. Pour the flour mixture into the middle of the baking dish.
5. Place the peaches in the middle of the mixture.
6. Dust the top of the cobbler with sugar.
7. Bake for 45 minutes.

To serve:

1. Spoon out the cobbler and top with cream of your choice and blackberries.

"Delicious lunch."
Michael Dawson, Chaucer

Serves 12

For the pastry:
500g plain flour
1 teaspoon nutmeg
1 teaspoon cinnamon
250g unsalted butter, cut into cubes
Pinch of salt
1 tablespoon caster sugar

1 egg, lightly beaten, plus additional egg for glazing
Splash of milk (optional)

For the filling:
350g pumpkin, skin on
150g sweet potato
25g unsalted butter

350ml double cream
50ml full fat milk
1 teaspoon ground cinnamon
100g caster sugar
250g egg yolk
Three-quarter teaspoon ground nutmeg

Sweet potato and pumpkin tart

To make the pastry:

1. Use fingertips to rub together flour, nutmeg, cinnamon and butter till it resembles fine breadcrumbs. Stir in salt and sugar then add the egg.

2. Work the pastry together in the bowl, adding a splash of milk if the mixture seems too dry. Tip onto a floured work surface and knead lightly until you have a smooth firm ball of pastry. Wrap in clingfilm and refrigerate for an hour or so.

3. Preheat the oven to 180°C/350°F/Gas mark 4.

4. Roll the pasty out on a floured surface to about 0.5 cm thick. Use the pastry to line a 20 x 20cm pastry ring, letting it overhang the sides. Line the tart with greaseproof paper and weigh down with baking beans wrapped in foil, making sure they are at least 1cm above the rim of the pastry.

5. Bake the tart blind for 20 minutes then remove tart from the oven and remove the beans. Trim the edges neatly and paint the shells with the remaining beaten egg. Return to the oven for five minutes then open the oven door and leave for another five minutes.

6. Remove and allow to cool before taking the shell out of the ring.

To make the filling:

1. Smear the pumpkin and sweet potato with butter, wrap them in foil and bake in the already hot oven for an hour or until softened.

2. Purée the pumpkin and sweet potato flesh and push through a fine sieve. Allow to cool then turn the oven temperature down to 120°C/260°F/Gas mark 1.

3. Measure 300g of the purée then whisk it with cream, milk, cinnamon, sugar and egg yolks. Strain through a fine chinois (conical sieve).

4. Put the tart case back in its ring and carefully fill it almost to the top. Sprinkle evenly with the nutmeg then bake in the oven for 55 minutes.

5. Remove and allow to cool before slicing and serving.

"Fantastic cuisine."
Marc Roothooft, Belgian pool

"Thanks Andy, something to aspire to."
Steve Willis, Oxford

Serves 4

For the custard ice cream (requires an ice cream maker):
250ml whole milk
100g sugar
Quarter teaspoon salt
2 egg yolks, lightly beaten

500ml thick double cream
2 teaspoons vanilla extract

For the bananas in caramel:
150g caster sugar
230ml water
Juice of 1 orange

4 tablespoons white rum or Malibu
1 vanilla pod
1 cinnamon stick
2 star anise
4 large, just ripe bananas

Bananas in caramel rum syrup served with custard ice cream

To make custard ice cream:

1. Place milk in a saucepan and heat over low heat until milk becomes hot and bubbles.
2. Add sugar and salt and stir till they have dissolved.
3. Remove from heat and add 1-2 tablespoons of the hot milk to the egg yolks, mixing well.
4. Add more milk to eggs, increasing the temperature of egg mixture.
5. Pour egg mixture back into pan and continue to cook over low heat, stirring constantly, until it starts to thicken and reaches 60°C (use a thermometer to measure) – about 10-12 minutes.
6. Place the pan in a sink or basin full of ice water to cool down, continuing to stir.
7. When the custard is just barely warm, stir in the cream and vanilla. Refrigerate mixture until ready to use.
8. Pour this mixture through a strainer prior to placing into the ice cream maker. Follow manufacturer's instructions to complete the process.

To make bananas in caramel:

1. Put the sugar and two tablespoons of the water in a large shallow pan over a gentle heat, stirring until dissolved.
2. When the sugar syrup is clear, raise the heat and cook to a light caramel (about five minutes). Immediately remove from the heat, cool for two minutes then stir in the orange juice.
3. Mix in the rum and remaining water.
4. Slit the vanilla pod lengthways and add to the syrup with the whole spices.
5. Peel the bananas and halve lengthways. Place in a single layer in the pan and spoon on the caramel syrup, ensuring the bananas are fully covered as this will prevent them from changing colour.
6. Leave to soften for about 40 minutes before serving.

If you do not have an ice cream machine you can use a good quality bought custard ice cream.

"Great lunch, Andy."
Nick Giles, Edwin Coe LLP

Serves 4

500g packet shortcrust pastry
4 ripe pears (not hard), peeled with
stalks intact
Quarter teaspoon cardamom seeds
2 tablespoons muscovado sugar
6 dried prunes, finely chopped
3 dried figs, finely chopped
Milk, to glaze
Golden caster sugar, for sprinkling

Baked pear dumplings

1. Preheat oven to 200°C/400°F/Gas mark 6.
2. Divide the pastry into four and roll each piece into a circle about 20cm in diameter. Set aside a small portion for later.
3. Pull the stalk out of each pear and set aside.
4. Core the pears using an apple corer, ensuring that no seeds remain.
5. Crush the cardamom seeds using a pestle and mortar and mix with the sugar, prunes and dried figs.
6. Fill the pears with the prune and fig mixture.
7. Put a pear upright on each pastry circle and brush the edges of the pastry with water. Fold the pastry up around the pear, keeping the shape. Press to seal and trim off any excess. Brush with milk and sprinkle with caster sugar.
8. Make pastry leaves with the remainder of the pastry and stick to the top of each pear.
9. Place a reserved stalk in each pear.
10. Bake on a buttered baking sheet for 30 minutes until pastry is golden brown.

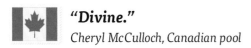

"Divine."
Cheryl McCulloch, Canadian pool

"Wonderful lunch, best for a long time."
Marie Vousey, London

Serves 6

50g softened butter
400-500g brioche loaf, sliced
60g mixed dried fruit
2 large eggs, plus 2 large yolks
40g caster sugar
300ml double cream

300ml milk
4 tablespoons Irish cream liqueur,
plus extra if needed
Demerara sugar, to sprinkle
3 tablespoons apricot jam

Brioche butter pudding

1. Preheat oven to 180°C/350°F/Gas mark 4.
2. Grease the sides of a 1.5-litre shallow ovenproof dish with the butter. Arrange the bread in the dish in overlapping layers, sprinkling the dried fruit in between.
3. Beat the whole eggs, egg yolks and sugar together in a large bowl until creamy, then beat in the cream, milk and liqueur. Slowly pour this over the bread and dried fruit.
4. Press the bread slices down gently with your fingers so they are completely submerged. Leave to stand for about 20 minutes to allow the bread to soak up the custard.
5. Stand the dish in a roasting tin and surround with boiling water to come halfway up the side of the dish. Sprinkle with demerara sugar and bake for 40-50 minutes until golden.
6. When this is nearly cooked, warm the apricot jam till runny. Dab this glaze over the surface of the pudding and leave to stand for 15 minutes before serving. The custard will stiffen during this time.
7. Additional liqueur can either be trickled on the pudding prior to serving or added in step 4 above.

"Great food as usual. Fantastic pudding!"
Barry Kemp, Willis

Serves 6

100g white chocolate
150g sponge of your choice (madeira etc)
3 fresh figs
500g fresh egg custard (from supermarket)

125g granulated sugar
6 tablespoons amaretto
2 tablespoons water
2 egg whites
Raspberries, silver balls or other toppings (optional)

Amaretto trifle with fig and toasted meringue

1. Break up and melt 100g white chocolate in a heatproof bowl over a pan of simmering water.
2. Remove from heat and stir until smooth.
3. Cool slightly.
4. Cut the sponge into small cubes and put into six serving glasses. Drizzle each with a tablespoon of amaretto.
5. Cut each fig into eight pieces and sit four pieces on top of sponge in each glass.
6. Gradually stir the fresh custard into the chocolate until thickened. Spoon into the glasses, then cover and chill until needed.
7. Put the granulated sugar and water into a heavy-based saucepan, bring slowly to boil and simmer gently for 15 minutes.
8. Meanwhile whisk the egg whites to a stiff peak.
9. Using an electric mixer, pour the hot syrup onto the egg whites in a steady stream while whisking until it is stiff and shiny. Cover with clingfilm.
10. Just before serving, spoon the meringue onto the custard.
11. Toast the tips of the meringue under a hot grill or with a blow torch for 30 seconds.
12. Sprinkle with raspberries, silver balls or toppings of your choice and serve.

Serves 6

45g caster sugar
3 medium eggs
100g plain flour, sifted
Pinch of salt
150ml full fat milk
50ml whipping cream
50ml water
2 teaspoons Kirsch (optional)
1 vanilla pod (optional)

40g butter, melted
500g whole cherries, washed and
pitted

To line the dish:
Melted butter
Caster sugar

To serve:
Icing sugar, for dredging

Cherry clafoutis

To make the batter:
1. Preheat oven to 180°C/350°F/Gas mark 4.
2. Beat sugar and eggs together until pale, then whisk in the flour and salt.
3. Gradually whisk in the milk, cream, water, kirsch and the seeds from the vanilla pod (if using), then stir in the melted butter.

For the cocottes (small ovenproof dishes):
1. Paint the insides of the cocottes with melted butter then sprinkle with sugar.
2. Fill the cocottes to about halfway with cherries then carefully pour the batter over them, about three-quarters of the way up the dish.
3. Bake for about 20 minutes or until the batter is puffed up and golden.
4. Dredge lightly with icing sugar and serve immediately.

Serves 6

For the crème d'amande:

100g butter, softened

200g caster sugar

100g ground almonds

100g ground macadamia nuts

20g plain flour

3 medium eggs

50ml dark rum (optional)

For the batter:

4 medium eggs

120g caster sugar

120g crème d'amande

120g crème fraîche, whipped

To serve:

Melted unsalted butter, for coating
the cocottes

Icing sugar, for coating and dredging
the cocottes

400g fresh blueberries

Blueberry flaugnarde

To make the crème d'amande:

1. In a mixer, beat the butter and sugar till pale and fluffy.
2. Beat in the almonds, macadamia nuts and flour.
3. Add the eggs one at a time, beating thoroughly each time.
4. Stir in the rum (if using).

To make the batter:

1. Beat the eggs and sugar together till pale.
2. Put the crème d'amande in a mixing bowl. Add the egg mixture, stirring in slowly.
3. Add the crème fraîche a little at a time and beat until the batter is smooth

To serve:

1. Preheat the oven to 180°C/350°F/Gas mark 4.
2. Paint the insides of the cocottes with melted butter then sprinkle with sugar.
3. Fill half way with blueberries, reserving a few.
4. Fill carefully with the batter to 2cm from the rim, then arrange the remaining blueberries over the top.
5. Bake for 20 minutes till golden.
6. Dredge with icing sugar and serve immediately.

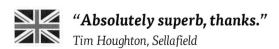

"Absolutely superb, thanks."
Tim Houghton, Sellafield

For the cake:
5 eggs, separated
165g sugar
192ml extra virgin olive oil
Juice from half a lemon
Zest from one lemon
160g self-raising flour, sifted
Butter, for greasing

For the raspberry syrup:
250g raspberries
125ml water
115g sugar
2 strips of lemon zest
1 strip of lime zest
1 strip of orange zest

For the lemon curd:
6 eggs
2 egg yolks
460g sugar
5 lemons, juice and zest
250g cold butter, cubed

Olive oil and lemon cake with raspberries

To make the cake:

1. Grease a 9-inch round cake tin with butter and line with parchment.
2. Preheat the oven to 180°C/350°F/Gas mark 4.
3. Beat the egg whites with the whisk attachment in an electric mixer on medium speed until light and frothy. Gradually add 55g sugar and continue whisking until soft peaks form. Transfer the whites to another bowl and set aside.
4. Add the egg yolks to the empty mixing bowl and beat on medium speed with the paddle attachment. Slowly add the remaining sugar, lemon juice and zest and beat until lightened in colour and thick.
5. With the mixer running, slowly drizzle in the olive oil in a steady stream. Then add the flour on a slow speed. When completely combined, remove bowl from the stand.
6. With a rubber spatula, scrape the sides of the bowl and stir in a third of the whisked egg whites. Slowly fold in the remaining egg whites, mixing gently until the mixture is combined. Pour into the prepared tin and bake for 35-40 minutes. The top of the cake should spring back when gently pressed.

To make the raspberry syrup:

1. Combine the sugar, zests and water in a saucepan and bring to a boil, dissolving the sugar.
2. When the syrup mixture thickens, add the raspberries and gently simmer till half the raspberries begin to pop and the syrup thickens.
3. Pour into a bowl, remove the zest and chill.

To make the lemon curd:

1. Combine all the ingredients, except the butter, in a mixing bowl. Place over a pot of simmering water and stir constantly with a wooden spoon or a heatproof spatula until thick.
2. Remove from the heat and stir in the butter, mixing until it is melted and combined.
3. Pour the mixture through a sieve into a clean bowl, cover the surface with clingfilm and chill.

To serve:

1. Put a slice of cake on a plate. Add lemon curd and raspberry syrup and serve.

Makes 30

For the pastry case:

500g plain flour, plus more for
kneading

Quarter teaspoon salt

185ml water, plus 2 tablespoons

450g unsalted butter, room
temperature, stirred until smooth

For the custard:

30g plain flour

310ml milk

330g granulated sugar

1 cinnamon stick

170ml water

Half teaspoon vanilla extract

6 large egg yolks, whisked

For the garnish:

Icing sugar, for dusting

Cinnamon, for dusting

You will need:

12 cup mini muffin tin

Egg custard tarts

For the pastry dough:

1. In a stand mixer fitted with a dough hook, mix the flour, salt, and water until a soft dough forms that pulls away from the sides.

2. Generously flour a work surface and pat the dough into a six-inch square using a pastry scraper. Flour the dough, cover with plastic wrap, and let it rest at room temperature for 15 minutes.

3. Roll the dough into an 18-inch square. As you work, use a scraper to lift the dough to make sure the underside is not sticking to your work surface.

4. Brush the excess flour off the top of the dough, trim any uneven edges, and, using a small offset spatula, dot and then spread the left two-thirds portion of the dough with a little less than one-third of the butter. Be careful to leave a one-inch plain border around the edge of the dough.

5. Neatly fold the unbuttered right third of the dough over the rest of the dough. Brush off any excess flour, then fold over the left third of the dough. Starting from the top, pat down the dough with your hand to release any air bubbles, and then pinch the edges of the dough to seal. Brush off any excess flour.

6. Turn the dough 90 degrees to the left so the fold is facing you. Lift the dough and flour the work surface. Once again roll it out to an 18-inch square, then dot the left two-thirds of the dough with a third of the butter and smear it over the dough. Fold the dough as directed in steps 4 and 5.

7. For the last rolling, turn the dough 90 degrees to the left and roll out the dough to an 18-by-21-inch rectangle, with the shorter side facing you. Spread the remaining butter over the entire surface of the dough.

8. Using the spatula as an aid, lift the edge of dough closest to you and roll it away from you into a tight log, brushing the excess flour from the underside as you go. Trim the ends and cut the log in half. Wrap each piece in plastic wrap and chill for two hours or preferably overnight.

Recipe continued overleaf.

Egg custard tarts (continued)

To make the custard:

1. In a medium bowl, whisk the flour and 60ml milk until smooth.

2. Bring the sugar, cinnamon, and water to a boil in a small saucepan and cook until water and sugar are combined – do not stir.

3. Meanwhile, in another small saucepan, scald the remaining 250ml milk. Whisk the hot milk into the flour mixture.

4. Remove the cinnamon stick and then pour the sugar syrup in a thin stream into the hot milk and flour mixture, whisking briskly. Add the vanilla and stir for a minute until very warm but not hot. Whisk in the yolks, strain the mixture into a bowl, cover with plastic wrap, and set aside.

To assemble and bake the pastries:

1. Preheat the oven to 230°C/450°F/Gas mark 8.

2. Remove a pastry log from the fridge and roll it back and forth on a lightly floured surface until it is about an inch in diameter and 16 inches long.

3. Cut it into two-centimetre pieces. Place one piece of the pastry dough, cut side down, in each well of a non-stick 12-cup mini muffin pan (allow the dough pieces to soften for several minutes until pliable).

4. Have a small cup of water nearby. Dip your thumbs in the water, then straight down into the middle of each dough spiral. Flatten them against the bottom of the cup to a thickness of about an eighth of an inch, then smooth the dough up the sides and create a raised lip just above the pan. The pastry sides should be thinner than the bottom.

5. Fill each cup three quarters full with the slightly warm custard. Bake the pastries until the edges of the dough are frilled and brown (about eight to nine minutes).

6. Remove from the oven and allow the pastries to cool a few minutes in the pan, then transfer to a rack and cool until just warm. Sprinkle the pastries generously with icing sugar and cinnamon and serve.

8. Repeat with the remaining pastry and custard. These are best eaten the day they are made.

"Delicious as always."
Eero Holma, Nordic pool

Serves 6-8

For the sweet shortcrust pastry:
250g plain flour
100g chilled butter, cubed, plus extra
for greasing
25g caster sugar
1 free-range egg, yolk and white
separated

For the pastry cream:
5 large free-range egg yolks

110g caster sugar
30g plain flour
Half teaspoon ground cinnamon
Pinch of salt
425ml milk
Vanilla pod
250ml double cream
1 tablespoon vanilla extract
2 tablespoons sweet sherry
2 tablespoons granulated sugar

For the topping:
375g raspberries
2 tablespoons redcurrant jelly
2 tablespoons hot water (just boiled)
Fresh mint, to garnish (optional)
Edible violas flowers, to garnish
(optional)

You will need:
25cm round tart tin with removable
ring

Raspberry and sherry tart

1. To make the pastry, place the flour, butter and sugar into a bowl. Gently and quickly rub the ingredients together into the consistency of breadcrumbs.

2. Lightly beat the egg yolk and drizzle it into the flour crumbs. Use a knife to mix through until the crumb starts to come together.

3. Using your hands, flatten the dough to about 2cm thick.

4. Wrap in clingfilm and refrigerate for 30 minutes.

5. Grease a 25cm round tart tin with butter and leave the tin to chill in the fridge.

6. When you are ready to roll out the pastry, remove it from the fridge and place between two large sheets of clingfilm. Roll out with a rolling pin until 3mm thick and until the circle formed is big enough to line the base and side of the tart tin.

7. Remove the top layer of clingfilm. Take the cooled tart tin from the fridge. Slide your hand palm up under the bottom layer of clingfilm with the pastry on top. Flip the pastry over onto the tart tin and gently lower into the base and using your thumb lightly push into the edges. Then use your thumb to 'cut' the pastry along the rim of the tin.

8. Remove the clingfilm and prick the pastry base with a fork. Chill the pastry and tin in the fridge while you heat the oven to 180°C/350°F/Gas mark 4.

9. To blind bake the pastry, remove the pastry and tart tin from the fridge. Cut a piece of greaseproof paper that is larger than the tin and scrunch into a ball and open out again so that it's soft and less rigid.

10. Place the paper into the pastry case and gently fill with baking beans. Bake blind in the oven for around 15-20 minutes, until it feels dry to the touch.

11. Remove the greaseproof paper and beans, brush the pastry with egg white and return to the oven for 5-8 minutes to seal the pastry.

Recipe continued overleaf.

Raspberry and sherry tart (continued)

To make the pastry cream:

1. Place the egg yolks and caster sugar in a bowl. Whisk until thick and pale in colour then stir in the flour, cinnamon and a pinch of salt.

2. Place the milk in a saucepan. Take the vanilla pod and score down the length with a knife add the pod to the milk and bring to the boil. Remove from the heat and leave the mixture to infuse for ten minutes.

3. Remove the vanilla pod and then slowly add the hot milk to the egg mixture, whisking all the time. Pour the mixture back into the pan and reduce the heat to low. Whisk constantly and bring to the boil again. After around two minutes the mixture should thicken. Pour into a cold bowl to stop the cooking process.

4. Whisk the cream until soft peaks form when the whisk is removed. Add the vanilla extract, sherry and sugar and mix them in. Then fold the cream into the pastry cream mixture and chill.

5. To assemble the tart, spoon the cooled pastry cream into the pastry case and top with raspberries. Dissolve the redcurrant jelly into the just boiled water to make a glaze. Using a pastry brush, gently coat the raspberries with the glaze.

6. To serve, remove the outer ring of the tin. Ease the base off with a knife and slide onto a plate or cake stand

7. Garnish with fresh mint and violas.

For the tart dough:
125g plain flour
45g granulated sugar
Half teaspoon salt
90g chilled butter, in small pieces
1 egg yolk beaten with 2 teaspoons
rosewater

For the filling:
115g sliced natural (raw) almonds,
plus more for sprinkling
1 tablespoon plain flour
90g granulated sugar
115g butter
2 eggs
Half teaspoon almond extract

Half teaspoon vanilla extract
350g pitted cherries
Icing sugar, for dusting

Cherry frangipane tart

1. First, make the tart base by mixing the flour, sugar and salt in a bowl. Rub butter into the mix till it resembles fine breadcrumbs.

2. Add the egg yolk and knead gently to form a soft smooth dough. Roll into a large circle and lay it in a 10-inch fluted tart tin with a removable bottom. Press in well and refrigerate for an hour.

3. Preheat oven to 220°C/425°F/Gas mark 7.

4. Bake blind till shell is lightly browned (about 10–15 minutes).

5. Whilst base is cooking, put almonds, flour and sugar in a food processor and grind to a rough powder. Add butter and pulse until fully blended.

6. Add eggs, almond and vanilla extract and blend until smooth and creamy.

7. Pour almond batter into the prebaked shell and smooth with a spatula.

8. Press cherries into the batter in a single layer. Sprinkle with a handful of sliced almonds.

9. Lower oven temperature to 190°C/375°F/gas mark 5 and bake until golden (about 35 minutes).

10. Remove from oven and cool on a rack. Remove from tin.

11. Serve with a dusting of icing sugar (you can flavour the icing sugar with almonds etc prior to dusting).

Makes 24

300g whipping cream

35g sorbitol powder

50g glucose

8g freshly ground coffee

300g Callebaut 811NV

400g Callebaut 823NV

40g unsalted butter, softened

Espresso coffee ganache

1. Bring the cream, sorbitol and glucose to the boil.
2. Add freshly ground coffee and infuse for five minutes. Pass through a sieve.
3. Pour onto pre-crystallised 811NV and 823NV chocolates. Stir in the butter.
4. Blend together to create an emulsion. Pour into a frame (1cm in thickness) and allow to crystallise overnight.
5. Spread a thin layer of pre-crystallised chocolate on one side of the ganache. Cut into desired shape.
6. Hand-dip the individual chocolates into pre-crystallised Callebaut 811NV dark chocolate.

Makes 24

130g whipping cream

130g raspberry coulis

1 capsule saffron fibres (0.5g)

650g Callebaut 823NV milk chocolate

Ganache of saffron and raspberry

1. Boil together the cream, raspberry coulis and saffron fibres.
2. Pass through a sieve onto the pre-crystallised 823NV milk chocolate. Blend together to create an emulsion.
3. Pour into a frame (1cm in thickness) and allow to crystallise overnight.
4. Spread a thin layer of pre-crystallised chocolate on one side of the ganache. Cut into desired shape.
5. Hand-dip the individual chocolates into pre-crystallised Callebaut 823NV milk chocolate.

Makes 24

175g whipping cream

30g glucose

500g Callebaut honey milk chocolate

35g unsalted butter, softened

Honey ganache

1. Boil the cream and glucose.
2. Pour onto pre-crystallised honey milk chocolate flavoured callets. Blend together to make an emulsion.
3. Cool to 35°C.
4. Stir in the butter and pour into a prepared tray or frame. Allow to crystallise overnight.
5. Spread a thin layer of pre-crystallised chocolate on one side of the ganache and cut into desired shape. Hand dip chocolates into pre-crystallised chocolate.

Index of Recipes (A-Z):

Lamb shanks with coolea pumpkin, 102
Lemon cake, 156
Lemon meringue tartlets, 148

Mixed flour baguettes, 46
Moules mariniere, 80
Multicoloured macaroons, 146

Olive oil and lemon cake with raspberries, 174
Olive oil bread, 42
Ostrich burger with potato wedges and red cabbage coleslaw, 124

Peach cobbler, 160
Peppered fillet steak, 130
Pheasant kiev with pancetta stack, 132
Pork loin with black pudding, 122
Pumpkin seed bread, 44

Raspberry and sherry tart, 179
Razor clams, 78
Red mackerel with gooseberry and ginger sauce, 64
Roast loin of kudu with savoury figs, 96
Roast monkfish with onions and purple potatoes, 74
Roast partridge with black garlic and sweet potato terrine, 126
Roast quail with leeks, red onion and mushroom, 128
Roasted wild sea bass with celeriac purée and braised fennel, 54
Rum and vanilla canelés, 150
Russian black bread, 38

Salmon trout poached in olive oil with cucumber and dill, 84
Simple linguine with garlic, squid and prawns, 52
Smoked haddock with spinach and egg, 72
Spicy prawns, 90
Steamed fillet of brill with green-lipped mussels, 82
Stir-fried salt and pepper squid, 70
Sunflower seed bread, 36
Sweet potato and pumpkin tart, 161

Three flavour focaccia, 48
Thyme and rosemary lamb, 106
Trifle, 142
Turbot on parsnip purée with a fresh herb dressing, 62

Veal wellington in port sauce with watercress purée, 99
Venison and potato cake with a fruity sauce, 116

Warm guinea fowl salad, 112

Contact Andrew Maddix:
thenuclearchef@hotmail.com